Living In Godliness

Living In Godliness

∮

"And without controversy great is the mystery of godliness: God was manifest in the flesh, justified in the spirit,seen of angels, preached unto the Gentiles, believed on in the world, received up in Glory."

First Timothy 3:16 (KJV)

Flora O. Erome-Utunedi

"Physical training is good, but training for godliness is much better, promising benefits in this life and in the life to come."

1 Timothy 4:8 (NLT)

ISBN-13: 9781546666813
ISBN-10: 1546666818

Contents

Foreword

§

IN A CHANGING WORLD WHERE absolutes are being done away with and truth is being disregarded, the call for holiness and righteousness is very important. This book challenges you to come back to the truth of God's Word and live a life pleasing to Him. With scripture as your foundation you will be encouraged to stand when others do not.

Rev. Mark Williams
Lead Pastor BP Church | Calgary AB

I find it refreshing that the discussion in this book focuses on believers living a godly life. In our western culture this subject is often down-played if not ignored. As you read this book you will appreciate the journey that Flora takes us on as she deals with the importance of godly living as taught by Paul. This book deals with godliness in the life of church leaders and lay leaders alike and the impact that godliness will have on their families underlined by the fact that the One who has called leaders is holy, and that is Jesus Christ.

As you read this book the author takes time to emphasize that living a godly life is totally dependent on Jesus and the power of Holy Spirit who lives in the lives of every believer. In this book, Flora takes time to develop how a believer's godly life will impact how leaders lead, how they will preach God's Word and how they produce true disciples.

You will discover truths that are shared from God's Word in this book; it is designed to bring us closer to God so we can be an instrument that God can use to draw us closer to Himself. I recommend that you take the time to prayerfully read the contents of this book which will challenge you to a life of godly living.

Pastor Noral Woodburn | BP Church

"Living in Godliness" gives us a clarion call to faithfully live out the high calling that Christ has for every believer. In our culture, where Christians can be tempted to live a life unworthy of their calling, Flora offers fresh insights and challenges on godly living and how we can commit ourselves once again to living a Christ-centered life anchored in His Word.

Rev. Brandon Sarney | BP Church
Associate Pastor

Acknowledgments

§

I AM INDEED VERY GRATEFUL to God Almighty for the privilege given to me to write this book, *"Living in Godliness."* This book is dedicated to God Almighty for revealing to humankind that it is possible to live in godliness. I acknowledge the Lord God Almighty for His greatness. "Yours O Lord is the greatness, the power, the glory, the victory, and the majesty. Everything in the heavens and on earth is yours. O Lord, and this is your kingdom. We adore you as the one who is over all things" (1 Chron. 29:11)(NLT).

I am thankful to my husband, Engineer/Deacon Erome Utunedi, and our children for their wonderful support during the writing of this book.

I would like to thank my Pastors, Mark Williams, Brandon Sarney, and Noral Woodburn of Beddington Pentecostal Church Calgary, for their kind support, prayers, and encouragement. I would also like to give special thanks to the Women's Prayer Ministry of Beddington Pentecostal Church for their prayers and support. Sincere thanks to all who supported and encouraged me.

My appreciation goes to the team of CreateSpace Publishing Company, for their invaluable help in publishing this book.

God bless you all.

Summary

§

LIVING IN GODLINESS IS A lifestyle of reverential fear and honor for God; a lifestyle that has been changed and transformed to line up with God's character. For Christians whose lives have been changed and transformed, this will take place by recognizing the lordship and the kingship of Jesus Christ. These Christians have been transformed from the old style of living to a new life in Christ Jesus. It is a spiritual mandate for the church of the living God to exercise godliness by faith through Jesus Christ.

Faith is complete trust in God and becomes active by taking a step to exercise godliness. This exercise is a continuous spiritual training that enhances and improves God-fearing Christians to walk in accordance with God's Word. These Christians are devoted, dedicated, and committed in their services to God Almighty. They are fully dedicated in their spiritual journey for God's work. These people of God train with His Word daily because they believe every part of the Word of God in order to become like Christ.

Spiritual training is abiding under the principles and righteousness of Jesus Christ, who lived by God's standard. This standard was set by the Word of God. Exercising godliness helps a Christian to be spiritually mature and productive, which means bearing spiritual fruits that represent true repentance. Matthew 3:8 (NLT) says: "Prove by the way you live that you have repented of your sins and turned to God." A Christian cannot do this kind of exercise without relying on God to transform and renew his or her mind. The Holy Spirit helps a transformed and renewed mind to produce good fruits. As a tree is identified by the fruits it produces, so are Christians identified by their fruits in the way they live. Matthew 12:33 (NLT) Says: "A tree is identified by its fruit. If a tree is good, its fruit will be good. If a tree is bad, its fruit will be bad."

Thank God for His grace that is more powerful than anything that can be imagined, to help the redeemed to live in godliness, which is the fruit of righteousness. Spirit-led life is an evidence of those who belong to Christ. These followers of Jesus Christ have nailed the sinful nature of their passions and desires on the cross which Christ was crucified. Living in godliness produces the fruits of the Holy Spirit. Galatians 5:22–25 (NLT) says:

"But the Holy Spirit produces this kind of fruit in our lives: love, joy, peace, patience, kindness, goodness, faithfulness, gentleness, and self-control. There is no law against these things! Those who belong to Christ Jesus have nailed the passions and desires of their sinful nature to his cross and crucified them there. Since we are living by the Spirit, let us follow the Spirit's leading in every part of our lives."

Living in godliness would have been impossible without the help of the grace of God. Human effort without His grace is fruitless because the grace of God actually disciplines the godly to stay away from sin to exercise godliness. Living in holiness is exercising godliness. The Word of God says, "Without holiness no one will see the Lord." Hebrews 12:14 (NIV) says: "Make every effort to live in peace with everyone and to be holy; without holiness no one will see the Lord."

The grace of God sets Christians apart to enable them to pursue godliness. God-fearing Christians unrelentingly pursue godliness with the help of the Holy Spirit for spiritual growth. A Spirit-led life is totally dependent on God to teach and to correct.

The Spirit-led life is God-fearing Christians who do not take the grace of God for granted to indulge in sinful acts. They train and exercise by applying the Word of God in every instance. Godly training is abiding under the principles of the Word of God and Christ's righteousness. Physical training is good for the body to keep fit, but training for godliness is much better for both physical and spiritual needs.

1 Timothy 4:8 (NLT) Says: "Physical training is good, but training for godliness is much better, promising benefits in this life and in the life to come." The benefits of living in godliness are not for this life alone, but in the life to come, which means spending eternity with Christ. God approves and delights with those who live for Him. Daily spiritual exercise occurs by studying and practicing the Word of God. It is therefore recommended for spiritual growth, which will lead to godliness.

Living in godliness is like an umbrella for divine covering and protection for Christians. Godliness is a lifestyle that is the outcome of a Christian who is truly born again and walks according to the leading of the Holy Spirit. A Christian cannot claim to be born again and still continue to live in sin and walk in darkness. 1 John 1:6 (NIV) says: "If we claim to have followership with him and yet walk in darkness, we lie and do not live out the truth."

Any born-again individual has fellowship with Christ. The lifestyle of the individual will reflect from the heart that Christ has transformed. God's people have a relationship and intimacy with God on a daily basis and this is reflected in their way of life. They have been washed and purified in the blood of the Lamb and have surrendered their heart and soul to God. They love God with their mind, soul, strength, and whole heart.

Living in godliness is abiding under the divine umbrella of God, in which Christ is the center. Training for godliness is doing what is right and acceptable in the sight of God at all times. These followers of Christ walk in obedience, and in accordance with God's Word, the armor a Christian needs daily to stand firm.

As an umbrella is used as a protection against the rain or the sun, living in godliness provides us a shield against every devices of the enemy. That does not mean a true follower of Christ will not have trouble, but the Lord guarantees His children's safety and protection to deliver them. " Psalms 34:19 (NIV) says: "The righteous person may have many troubles, but the Lord delivers him from them all;"

It is important that Christ's followers must pursue godliness with a sincere heart, believing and trusting in the finished work of Jesus Christ. Living in godliness is wearing the whole armor of God through Christ. God empowered His children to live their full spiritual potentials when they abide in Him; to withstand the enemy in the evil days and to live a victorious life in Christ Jesus. God's people are encouraged to guard their loins with the belt of truth, the Word of God, and to put on the breastplate of righteousness to resist the enemy, according to Ephesians 6:13–14 (NLT) says: "Therefore, put on every piece of God's armor so you will be able to resist the enemy in the time of evil. Then after the battle you will still be standing firm. Stand your ground, putting on the belt of truth and the body armor of God's righteousness."

Walking according to the will of God with faith and believing in His Word plays an important role in living in godliness. A Christian with a godly lifestyle acts upon the Word of God by the way he or she lives, trusting in God's Will in every situation. Living in godliness is a continuous walk and exercise of faith in God until Christ returns for His church, the hope of glory. Philippians 3:12–21 (NLT) says:

"I don't mean to say that I have already achieved these things or that I have already reached perfection. But I press on to possess that perfection for which Christ Jesus first possessed me. No, dear brothers and sisters, I have not achieved it, but I focus on this one thing: Forgetting the past and looking forward to what lies ahead, I press on to reach the end of the race and receive the heavenly prize for which God, through Christ Jesus, is calling us. Let all who are spiritually mature agree on these things. If you disagree on some point, I believe God will make it plain to you. But we must hold on to the progress we have already made. Dear brothers and sisters, pattern your lives after mine, and learn from those who follow our example. For I have told you often before, and I say it again with tears in my eyes, that there are many whose conduct shows they are really enemies of the cross of Christ. They are headed for destruction. Their god is their appetite, they brag about shameful things, and they think only about this life here on earth. But we are citizens of heaven, where the Lord Jesus Christ lives. And we are eagerly waiting for him to return as our Savior. He will take our weak mortal bodies and change them into glorious bodies like his own, using the same power with which he will bring everything under his control."

God's people live as citizens of heaven through their conduct. These Christians have their focus in Christ alone and are not involved in self-indulgence. Their lives have been patterned after Jesus Christ. Living in godliness is the living standard for Christianity. Jesus Christ's righteousness alone is what the believers depend on through their walk with God by faith. The godly live with the mind-set of the kingdom of God for the return of Christ, as citizens of heaven.

Godliness is the spiritual garment for those who live in Christ Jesus by applying His Word on a daily basis, which leads to righteous living. It is impossible to live a righteous life without practicing a godly lifestyle. When a Christian pursues godliness, it enables him or her to live in full spiritual potentials. Spiritual maturity comes from studying the Word of God and acting upon it. The godly are rooted in the Word of God because they are connected in their walk with God. They flourish in and out of season because they have harmony with God. They rely and depend on God Almighty for all their expectations.

Christ followers who by His Grace have come to know Him will grow in the knowledge of God by their conduct. Colossians 1:10 (NLT) says: "Then the way you live will always honor and please the Lord, and your lives will produce every kind of good fruit. All the while, you will grow as you learn to know God better and better." God's people live a godly lifestyle by exercising and walking out their faith by His Word.

Brothers and sisters, you are encouraged to pursue righteousness with the love of God in whatever you do to live a productive life. The Bible declares that the godly are those who delight and meditate in the law of the Lord. God's people are blessed because they walk in the ways of the Lord. Living in godliness means abstaining from evil, and the Bible describes people living godly lives as being like trees planted by the rivers of water, "Whatever they do shall prosper." Psalms 1:1–6 (NLT) says:

> "Oh, the joys of those who do not follow the advice of the wicked, or stand around with sinners, or join in with mockers. But they delight in the law of the Lord, meditating on it day and night. They are like trees planted along the riverbank, bearing fruit each season. Their leaves never wither, and they prosper in all they do. But not the wicked! They are like worthless chaff, scattered by the wind. They will be condemned at the time of judgment. Sinners will have no place among the godly. For the Lord watches over the path of the godly, but the path of the wicked leads to destruction."

God's love and the righteousness upon the godly motivate them to produce good works. The love of God is not for selfish gain, but to bring glory to God Almighty. Believers should recognize that Christ has given His promises to His church to share in His divine nature with everything the church needs to live in godliness. God has already made provision of moral excellence for the church to have knowledge of how to live in a godly lifestyle. Godly life is the application of the Word of God daily to help Christians to be active and effective throughout their spiritual journey.

Apostle Peter also emphasized that believers should supplement their faith with a generous provision of moral excellence on how to live a godly life. Practicing godliness will enable a Christian to grow to be more like Christ, more productive and useful in the service of God. Living in godliness is looking beyond this world and run with purpose to win the eternal prize that God prepared for His church. 1 Corinthians 9:25–26 (NLT) says: "All athletes are disciplined in their training. They do it to win a prize that will fade away, but we do it for an eternal prize. So I run with purpose in every step. I am not just shadowboxing."

Apostle Peter is reminding the church again that faith was given to the church through Jesus Christ because of God's justice and fairness—that is, those who believe in Him will share in His promise by the finished work of Christ on the cross. Living a new life means forgetting the past of your old ways by repenting from every kind of sin. God promised the church that we would share in His divine nature. That was why He died for all. Those who accept Christ into their life and walk according to His Word will escape this world's corruption caused by human desires.

Godliness is the key to operate in the divine nature of God as His children. God's people are spiritually intelligent and can sense if things are not right, no matter how a situation is presented. They sense with their spirits because they have the mind of Christ. That is why a Christian must make every effort to grow in the knowledge of His Word to be productive and useful in the services of God.

According to 2 Peter 1:1–9 (NLT) says:

"This letter is from Simon Peter, a slave and apostle of Jesus Christ. I am writing to you who share the same precious faith we have. This faith was given to you because of the justice and fairness of Jesus Christ, our God and Savior. May God give you more and more grace and peace as you grow in your knowledge of God and Jesus our Lord. By his divine power, God has given us everything we need for living a godly life. We have received all of this by coming to know him, the one who called us to himself by means of his marvelous glory and excellence. And because of his glory and excellence, he has given us great and precious promises. These are the promises that enable you to share his divine nature and escape the world's corruption caused by human desires. In view of all this, make every effort to respond to God's promises. Supplement your faith with a generous provision of moral excellence, and moral excellence with knowledge, and knowledge with self-control, and self-control with patient endurance, and patient endurance with godliness, and godliness with brotherly affection, and brotherly affection with love for everyone. The more you grow like this, the more productive and useful you will be in your knowledge of our Lord Jesus Christ. But those who fail to develop in this way are short sighted or blind, forgetting that they have been cleansed from their old sins."

Godliness is a lifestyle of the faithful Christian who genuinely follows the principles and doctrine of Jesus Christ. These Christians are devoted to God and His teachings, the only truth that leads to godliness. God's Word is the written instructions and principles that guide Christians to live in godliness. A Christian life is reflected in God's Word alone. John 17:17 (NLT) says: "Make them holy by your truth; teach them your word, which is truth."

The truth is that the Word of God is the only source that transforms the heart of a Christian to live a holy life. Christians who genuinely want to live a godly life run away from evil. To have knowledge of His Word without living in godliness is like building a house on a false foundation. That kind of dwelling will collapse because it's like reading a manual without application. It will be difficult for a ministry or Christian to function spiritually without living out the Word of God.

Jesus Christ's ministry was all about the kingdom of God, preaching the good news and repenting from sins. True repentance brings genuine change of heart and behavior in the life of a Christian. A Christian's life is transformed from within to live in godliness and holiness because of what Jesus Christ did on the cross. The way a Christian lives proves he or she has truly repented by his or her actions by turning away from willful and deliberate sin.

The Bible makes it clear that the people of God admonished one another daily about the consequences of sin. A Christian should make sure his or her heart is not evil and unbelieving by turning away from the living God. Christians are encouraged to be faithful and trust God to the end. Hebrews 3:12–15 (NLT) says:

> "Be careful then, dear brothers and sisters. Make sure that your own hearts are not evil and unbelieving, turning you away from the living God. You must warn each other every day, while it is still "today," so that none of you will be deceived by sin and hardened against God. For if we are faithful to the end, trusting God just as firmly as when we first believed, we will share in all that belongs to Christ. Remember what it says: "Today when you hear his voice, don't harden your hearts as Israel did when they rebelled."

Repentance is the key to start living in godliness. The godly are God-fearing individuals who press on by God's grace to live by His own standard through the power of the Holy Spirit. Their lifestyle and faith are genuine because they do not contradict what they preach and do. According to 2 Corinthians 13:5 (NLT) says: "Examine yourselves to see if your faith is genuine. Test yourselves. Surely you know that Jesus Christ is among you; if not, you have failed the test of genuine faith."

Christians are encouraged to examine themselves daily with the Word of God and let their lifestyles influence others positively. Living in godliness helps a Christian to be loyal and faithful to God in his or her ministry, including in how he or she spends God's money. Christians depend solely on the Word of God, which they preach and apply to their personnel lives. They are sincere and truthful in their calling to deliver their work as true servants of God.

True Christianity is living a godly life from the perspective of the Word of God, in a behavior that is consistent with His Word. Consistency with the Word of God is very important when it comes to living a godly lifestyle. The behavior of a Christian has to agree with the values and principles of God's Word. These Christians are stable and firm in their faith in Jesus Christ. The Word of God has transformed and shaped their hearts to be more like Christ. The effect of His Word in the life of a Christian over a period of time brings uniformity in the pattern of how a Christian should live.

Integrity matters so much for true followers of Christ because they are Christ ambassadors, which means they act upon the Word of God with clear biblical directives that lead to godliness. They are able to discern when things are not right because they are in obedience to God's instructions. Working in the vineyard of God by serving others and doing other things in the name of the Lord without living a lifestyle of godliness is a life of deception and of living in a false hope.

CHAPTER 1

Introduction

§

1.1 GODLINESS

GODLINESS IS A LIFESTYLE OF a Christian living that is consistent with the Word of God. Without the experience of a spiritual birth through Christ, living in godliness would be impossible. The spiritual birth means to be born again by the power of the Holy Spirit into the family of God. This spiritual birth is an experience that happens when a person accepts Jesus Christ as his or her Lord and personal Savior. This experience brings change and transformation in the life of a person who sincerely repents from sin. His or her heart and mind has now become renewed because he or she has decided to turn away from their old ways to a new way of living in Christ Jesus.

These God's people now live dedicated lives, devoted and faithful to God Almighty. The Holy Spirit has taken over their hearts and minds so that they can experience a new life that is in Christ Jesus because they have a holy fear for God in their heart. These Christians are faithful, consistent, and genuine. They serve God with joy in the fullness of the Holy Spirit. Their eternal joy does not come by feelings or possession of what they have. It is the gifts of the Holy Spirit that comes with the power of the salvation of their soul. This is the kind of eternal joy that drives the godly to preach the good news without being wrongly motivated. They are passionate about God Almighty. Their top priority is all about God's agenda to work for Him.

Most importantly God guides these Christians with His abundance of grace as they walk with Him in obedience. 2 Timothy 2:15–16 (NLT) says: "Work hard so you can present yourself to God and receive his approval. Be a good worker, one who does not need to be ashamed and who correctly explains the word of truth. Avoid worthless, foolish talk that only leads to more godless behavior."

The heart of God for all Christians is to do His will, not ours. The key to the heart of God is always to please Him—that is, to do His will. Jesus Christ only recognizes Christians who do God's will. These followers of Christ are not involved in self-indulgence and self-pleasing. Jesus Christ said clearly in His words that only those who do the will of God the Father will enter the kingdom of God. Matthew 7:21–23 (NLT) says:

> "Not everyone who says to me, "Lord, Lord," will enter the kingdom of heaven, but only the one who does the will of my Father who is in heaven. Many will say to me on that day, "Lord, Lord, did we not prophesy in your name and in your name drive out demons and in your name perform many miracles?" Then I will tell them plainly, "I never knew you. Away from me, you evildoers!"

The above statement said by Jesus Christ, "I never knew you," says a lot and sends a very strong message to every Christian. "I never knew you" means they were working for themselves, not God. These Christians were involved in using the name of Jesus Christ to work without God's approval because they were not doing His will. They have fellowship with other Christians without a genuine repentance and conviction of sins in their lives.

If a person is not convicted of sin, there will be no total conversion. When there is no conviction of sin, the individual will be working in his or her own strength and effort to be recognized by people, not Jesus Christ. To be recognized and known by God, according to the Bible, Christians must genuinely repent to be born again. A

Christian who is converted from the kingdom of darkness to the kingdom of light must follow the ways of God, not his or her own way. Christ followers must surrender to God and turn away from evil and sin. God only knows the work of a Christian if it is genuine. People can be deceived, but God cannot be. The Bible says God can never be mocked. Galatians 6:7 (KJV) says: "Be not deceived; God is not mocked: for whatever a man soweth, that shall he also reap."

Any church meeting, mission, ministry, teaching, or gathering that is not ordained or recognized by God is wasted effort and time. Brothers and sisters, let's examine ourselves daily with the Word of God to see that our effort and work are genuine. Godliness is living a Christ-like life and doing God's will. The will of a Christian must align with His will. The godly show a real change in their conduct and their daily lifestyle as followers of Jesus Christ.

The Word of God is the only source that can mold a believer's character to be godly. The Word of God is the perfect mirror to look at daily to examine oneself. Christianity without living in godliness is like running a race without a goal. From the Bible point of view, God gave an instruction to the church to be holy in every aspect of life. God paid a ransom to save humanity—not to live the way we want but to live for Him alone. The precious blood of Jesus Christ is the one and only source that is powerful enough to cleanse any kind of sin.

When sin is confessed and repented from, God is willing to forgive. Good work without godly repentance is like building on a false foundation. Good work without Christ is self-righteousness that comes from human effort, while the righteousness of God comes only from Christ by depending on Him and doing His will. Through faith in God, the godly can live holy lives in Christ Jesus. 1 Peter 1:15–21 (NLT) says:

"But now you must be holy in everything you do, just as God who chose you is holy. For the Scriptures say, "You must be holy because I am holy." And remember that the heavenly

Father to whom you pray has no favorites. He will judge or reward you according to what you do. So you must live in reverent fear of him during your time here as temporary residents. For you know that God paid a ransom to save you from the empty life you inherited from your ancestors. And it was not paid with mere gold or silver, which lose their value. It was the precious blood of Christ, the sinless, spotless Lamb of God. God chose him as your ransom long before the world began, but now in these last days he has been revealed for your sake. Through Christ you have come to trust in God. And you have placed your faith and hope in God because he raised Christ from the dead and gave him great glory."

God paid the price with the blood of Jesus Christ to set people free from the captivity of sin to live godly and holy lives. Sin and evil must be repented from in order to experience the freedom. The power in the blood of Jesus Christ is able to purify and sanctify any person who truly repents from sin. Repentance and obedience opens the door for the Holy Spirit to work in the lives of Christians to enable them to live godly lives. Godliness is living a new life in Christ Jesus. Living in godliness is a true picture of what God has done in the life of a Christian, on the cross through Jesus Christ.

There must be a distinct behavioral difference that separates the godly from the ungodly. A truly repentant heart brings a genuine change of heart to live in godliness. The help of the Holy Spirit and a willing heart is the major key to living a godly lifestyle. The Word of God has the power to transform the heart of a believer to line up with God's character. That is why the Word of God must be close to the heart of a Christian so he or she doesn't imitate the ways and lifestyles of the ungodly.

Godliness is a total devotion to God's style of doing things. It will be difficult to live a godly life when a Christian fails to trust God and to rely on the leading of the Holy Spirit. The godly do not operate in the way they feel. The power of the Holy Spirit through faith leads them. It is true that God's grace saves Christians. Grace is not an excuse for disorderliness. The grace of God actually helps Christians not to go against the moral norms of His Word. God wants His church to live a godly and holy life with the right choice to live for Him. Jude 1:3–4 (NLT) says:

> "Dear friends, I had been eagerly planning to write to you about the salvation we all share. But now I find that I must write about something else, urging you to defend the faith that God has entrusted once for all time to his holy people. I say this because some ungodly people have wormed their way into your churches, saying that God's marvelous grace allows us to live immoral lives. The condemnation of such people was recorded long ago, for they have denied our only Master and Lord, Jesus Christ."

God's marvelous grace allows believers to live moral lives to defend the faith that God has entrusted to His holy people. Having faith in God alone without a godly repentance is a false hope. Honesty with godliness works together in the life of a believer in everything for a godly living. Proverbs 16:8 (NLT) says: "Better to have little, with godliness, than to be rich and dishonest."

Dishonesty can lead to lies, deceit, and fraud. The lifestyle of dishonesty does not reflect the Word of God and therefore must be repented from so God will forgive and restore you. Godliness brings contentment and honesty. Living in godliness is a great wealth and an asset to God-fearing people because it is the key to spiritual prosperity. 1 Timothy 6:6 (NLT) says: "Yet true godliness with contentment is itself great wealth."

Spiritual wealth for the true believers is the benefit of godly living. Godliness helps the believer to live a disciplined and Spirit-led life. Godliness is a spiritual exercise that the Christian practices every day to draw near to God by studying and applying His Word. By living in godliness, there must be a visible change and sincerity in the life of a Christian. The true picture of a Christian is to exercise godliness. These Christians are selfless and committed to preach the truth no matter what because they do not try to modify the Word of God for their personal gain. The gospel should not be preached for personal profit but to save souls for eternal life. 2 Corinthians 2:17 (NLT) says: "You see, we are not like the many hucksters who preach for personal profit. We preach the word of God with sincerity and with Christ's authority, knowing that God is watching us."

During the time of the apostles, the gospel was not preached, as if it were buying and selling commodities. The apostles genuinely preached about repentance and the loving mercies of Christ through the good news. They were focused on how Christians should live godly lifestyles. The message of godliness was constantly a reminder to the churches on how Christians should live a new life in Christ Jesus. The Bible says an old sinful nature has to be stripped off to live a complete new life in Christ Jesus. A change of heart and a lifestyle of a Christian should reflect true repentance, transparency, and genuine working for the Lord. Practicing the Word of God enables Christians to live in godliness. The grace of God is very powerful to change lives when individuals genuinely repent from their sin. Colossians 3:8–10 (NLT) says:

> "But now is the time to get rid of anger, rage, malicious behavior, slander, and dirty language. Don't lie to each other, for you have stripped off your old sinful nature and all its wicked deeds. Put on your new nature, and be renewed as you learn to know your Creator and become like him."

Living in godliness is a devoted lifestyle of a believer by feeding on the Word of God, the spiritual bread that is active and powerful in the life of the believer. The godly yearn and crave for this bread daily because it is the source of power through Christ by faith. Every day the godly learn to know the Creator by reading His Word to become like Him. Feeding on the spiritual bread daily will sustain and help the Christian to grow.

Christians, who focus on the physical food alone, without reading and applying His Word, will not grow spiritually. In fact, it will be difficult to live a godly life. The source of the power of a Christian is deriving from the Word of God by the power of the Holy Spirit. For those Christians who feed on the Word of God daily and walk according to His ways, their lives are productive daily because they are rooted in Christ, and they cannot stop producing good fruits. Jesus declares in His Word in Luke 4:4 (KJV), "And Jesus answered him, saying, It is written, That man shall not live by bread alone, but by every word of God."

When a Christian is faced with challenges, answers can only be found in the Word of God. True believers draw their strength from His Word to overcome—as Jesus Christ did to the devil. It is only the power in the Word of God that defeats the devil. Christian are encouraged to study the Word of God because it the sword of the Holy Spirit given to us by God that works within us. The Word of God is the key to lock and unlock doors in any situation.

When you invest your time to read and study the Word of God, it is like investing your money in the bank to use when the need arises. You are building on a solid foundation, which is in Jesus Christ, to stand on the evil day. Hallelujah! God has given the godly the sword of the Holy Spirit, which the Word of God, for victory.

CHAPTER 2

Godliness as an Acronym

2.1 GROW

GROW IS A PROCESS AS a result of studying His Word and applying it daily to increase in the knowledge of God. The Word of God helps Christians to grow spiritually into maturity as they walk with God in their Christian faith. Growing in Christian faith will involve intimacy with God, spending time to study His Word and to pray. An understanding of God's Word actually helps the godly to develop spiritually and have a close relationship with God.

Maturity in the Word of God plays an important role for spiritual growth. The biblical mandate for all true believers is to live out the Word of God, while the spiritual mandate is to represent Christ as an ambassador of the kingdom of God. Godliness comes by practicing and living out the Word of God by exercising Christian faith through Jesus Christ. The more a believer studies and reflects on the Word of God, the more his or her life and spiritual growth is affected. A Christian who is committed and dedicated to the Word of God is revealed in life as a follower of Jesus Christ, specifically in the manner the Christian loves, talks, dresses, and see things in God's own perspective.

Christians who have a very sound biblical knowledge of the Word of God are not easily deceived; they test every spirit. The spiritual growth of Christians gives them an understanding of His Word. Because of this growth, they can acknowledge the incredible greatness of God's power in every situation. The lifestyle of godliness equips God's people to be spiritually minded and able to recognize some of the tactics of the devil.

Lack of knowledge of the Word of God has made some Christians derail. The godly depend only on the one who is all-knowing and powerful, the Lord God Almighty, the Creator of the universe. The devil, to some extent, knows the Word of God, but he is not all-knowing and powerful. For those Christians who do not create time to read God's Word, the devil takes advantage of the situation to deceive many because these individuals lack the knowledge of the Word of God. The devil uses these tactics to lure many to sin. Reading the Word of God gives a Christian an understanding of who God is so he or she can understand the mind of God for His children.

With the lack of the knowledge of God's Word, some of these Christians have drifted away from the truth. That is why some are unable to recognize the lies and deception of the devil. With the help of the Holy Spirit and God's Word, the godly can discern when things are not right. The godly are able to recognize when the gospel is presented cleverly in such a way to sound like the truth. Christians are encouraged to read and study the Bible on a daily basis to grow in their faith and walk with God. 2 Peter 3:18 (NLT) says: "Rather you must grow in the grace and knowledge of our Lord and Savior Jesus Christ. All glory to him, both now and forever! Amen."

Followers of Jesus Christ read the Bible for spiritual wisdom and insight so they can grow in grace and the knowledge of God. Christ gave the various gifts to the church for the edification of His church to the glorification of God the Father. These spiritual exercises of the gifts help God's people to be mature in the Lord and to encourage one another. Ephesians 4:11–16 (NLT) says:

"Now these are the gift Christ gave to the church: the apostles, the prophets, the evangelists, and the pastors and teachers. Their responsibility is to equip God's people to do his work and build up the church, the body of Christ. This will continue until we all come to such unity in our faith and knowledge of God's Son that we will be mature in the Lord, measuring up to the full and complete standard of Christ. Then we will no longer be immature like children. We won't be tossed and blown about by every wind of new teaching. We will not be influenced when people try to trick us with lies so clever they sound like the truth. Instead, we will speak the truth in love, growing in every way more and more like Christ, who is the head of his body, the church. He makes the whole body fit together perfectly. As each part does its own special work, it helps the other parts grow, so that the whole body is healthy and growing and full of love."

Exercising godliness among believers in the Lord Jesus Christ brings spiritually healthy growth and a genuine love for God and to others. When the body of Christ is connected to the Lord spiritually, unity and spiritual nourishment flows from the throne of grace to the body of Christ. As a result, God's people will grow spiritually by practicing His Word to live in godliness. Colossians 2:7 (NLT) says:

"Let your roots grow down into him, and let your lives be built on him. Then your faith will grow strong in the truth you were taught, and you will overflow with thankfulness. Don't let anyone capture you with empty philosophies and high-sounding nonsense that come from human thinking and from the spiritual powers of this world, rather than from Christ."

God's Word overrides human philosophy and godless ideas because there is power in His Word. That is why it is possible to live in godliness. When a Christian reads the Word of God, the Holy Spirit helps to train him or her to grow spiritually to recognize the Word that is from God and also from human knowledge. Hebrews 5:13–15 (NLT) says: "For someone who lives on milk is still an infant and doesn't know how to do what is right. Solid food is for those who are mature, who through training have the skill to recognize the difference between right and wrong."

Spiritual growth and maturity comes with time for believers in the Lord Jesus Christ. Training and exercising the Word of God develops spiritual skills of a Christian to know the difference between right and wrong. It is a gradual process and a continuous walk with God to grow daily. A Christian will continue to grow spiritually until Jesus Christ returns for His church. Living in godliness is a continuous work in progress. By training with the Word of God, Christians develop spiritually and can thus recognize the difference between right and wrong. God's people recognize His voice and hear from Him to help them know the difference between evil and good.

Maturity in God's Word develops the spiritual senses of a child of God so that he or she can view situation in the way God sees it. They walk with the mind-set of Christ to evaluate all things. One of the ways God speaks, God reveals His MIND through His Word. 1 Corinthians 2:16 (NLT) says: "For, Who can know the LORD's thoughts? Who knows enough to teach him? But we understand these things, for we have the mind of Christ."

For Christians to grow, to have the mind of Christ, they must study to understand God's Word. God's people have the mind of Christ and function with spiritual wisdom from God because they walk according to His will. The secret behind doing the will of God is not just to grow spiritually, but it opens divine doors and equips God's people spiritually because it is the key to the heart of God. That is why, for the godly, their ultimate desire always is to please God. Hebrews 13:21 (NLT) says: "May he equip you with all you need for doing his will, through the power of Jesus Christ, every good thing that is pleasing to him. All glory to him forever and ever! Amen."

2.2 OBEDIENCE

Living in godliness is an act of obedience to God by complying with His Word. Obedience is willingness to do what God requires of His church by following His guidance through His Word. Obedience to God's Word means that God's opinion counts and should be taken more seriously than human opinion. This means obeying God wholeheartedly in your relationship and walk with Him.

Conformity in accordance with the Word of God in your action is living in godliness. Following God's way is living in obedience to follow His precepts. God's way is repenting and turning away from sin and evil by doing His will. Christ is calling out to His church to repent from every aspect they are still walking in disobedience to His Word. He wants His church to live a life of godliness. Christ's followers who choose to live a godly lifestyle must surrender to God totally by obeying Him. The grace of God is never an excuse for a Christian to continue in sin and indulge in evil deeds. Romans 6:15–19 (NLT) says:

> "Well then, since God's grace has set us free from the law, does that mean we can go on sinning? Of course not! Don't you realize that you become the slave of whatever you choose to obey? You can be a slave to sin, which leads to death, or you can choose to obey God, which leads to righteous living. Thank God! Once you were slaves of sin, but now you wholeheartedly obey this teaching we have given you. Now you are free from your slavery to sin, and you have become slaves to righteous living. Because of the weakness of your human nature, I am using the illustration of slavery to help you understand all this. Previously, you let yourselves be slaves to impurity and lawlessness, which led ever deeper into

sin. Now you must give yourselves to be slaves to righteous living so that you will become holy."

It is impossible for a Christian to please God without the complete control of the Holy Spirit in his or her life. Obedience to His Word is not just hearing the Word of God alone. It is all about doing and living out His Word. Obedience to the Word of God involves taking a step of faith to be disciplined by His Word with the help of the Holy Spirit to guide.

A slave to sin leads a life of lawlessness and impurity, and the reason for such lifestyle is nothing but compromise. Attitude toward the Word of God plays a major role in the life of a Christian either to live a godly or ungodly life. Some attitudes have made some Christians compromise the Word of God, which has led their first attempt of sin and leads them to go deeper into sin.

Please return to the Lord in obedience. He will forgive you. Being a slave to righteous living, humanly speaking, is a difficult task and exercise to do. But Jesus Christ is willing and able to help a Christian who has taken a conscious decision to obey God on a daily basis to live in godliness. The Bible is the inspired Word of God given as a guideline to everyone who believes in Him and wants to walk with Him in obedience.

2.3 DISCIPLE

A disciple is a follower of Jesus Christ who is devoted and committed to the teachings and the doctrines of Jesus Christ. Disciples do not just read or preach the Word. They lived a lifestyle of godliness. They are living epistles that people can read and know God through their lifestyle. Their primary assignment is to do the work of God, who calls them to bring glory to Him alone. Disciples' lifestyles are in accordance with God's Word.

Living in godliness means a dedicated life that the principles of the Word of God discipline. Disciples are faithful, selfless, diligent, dedicated, loving, caring, and truthful. Matthew 16:24 says, "Then Jesus said to his disciples, 'If any of you wants to be my follower, you must turn from your selfish ways, take up your cross, and follower me.'"

Jesus Christ made clear to His followers the conditions of discipleship, one of which is to be selfless. Disciples are to take up the cross and follow Him. Disciples must give up something to be a follower of Jesus Christ. Living in godliness is not self-centered life or selfish ways. Rather, it is giving up something for God to be in total control of your life.

Disciples are true representatives of the kingdom of God because they are ambassadors of Jesus Christ and citizens of heaven. These Christians operate in the spirit of truth and holiness to teach, preach, and pray. They also sacrifice their time for the things that matter most to God. These disciples know that time spent for God is an investment that is never wasted. Disciples who spend quality time with God get results, no matter how long it takes. They wait on God for answers. They persevere and endure trials and temptations that confront them through prayers. They depend on God by relying and trusting Him to come through for them by solving their problems.

Disciples know, in the decision to follow Jesus, the journey can be rough and bumpy at times, but their mind has already been made up not to give in to the deceit of the enemy, the devil. These disciples have full confidence in God and are very positive about Him. They follow Christ no matter the challenge that comes their way. They are not willing to give up. They are fearless with determination to follow Jesus Christ because they dearly love God. True disciples must have a genuine love for God and others. Their love for God is always their first priority before anything else. They will always represent the interest of Jesus Christ in their calling to fulfill their divine mandate. Disciples are faithful to the teachings of God's Word. They exercise the authority given to them by God standing upon His Word to whomever that needs it and not for commercial purpose.

God uses disciples to build spiritual lives to influence His kingdom. Disciples of Christ know the truth about God that He never fails from their experience in their walk with Him. Disciples are trained by God's Word to know and speak the truth. They live in godliness as a disciple of Christ, and the incorruptible Word of God makes the difference in their life. The Word of God is capable and powerful to bring changes in the life of anyone who believes to become a disciple. Changes occur when a disciple remains faithful and loyal to the teachings and doctrines of Jesus Christ to experience a life of freedom in Christ.

The truth about God's Word will help disciples not be ignorant about Satan's devices that come through deception and lies. John 8:31 (NLT) says: "Jesus said to the people who believed in him, "You are truly my disciples if you remain faithful to my teachings. And you will know the truth, and the truth will set you free."

Disciples are courageous, and they are bold to speak the truth of God's Word because they live by example. His Word is the only source of truth that the disciples depend on. They do not conspire to do evil but promote God's Word and rejoice in the truth. Disciples know the devil is consistent with his character of lying because he is the father of lies. That is why anyone who lives under the deception of the devil's lies will hate the truth.

The spiritual assignment for a disciple is to know and speak the truth in every situation at all times. Disciples preach in accordance with God's Word because they acknowledge that the final opinion and analysis is from God's own point of view from His Word. They don't preach what people want to hear; they preach what God is speaking through His Word. Christians should be known for speaking the truth at all times because it gladdens the heart of God.

A lie is an opposition to the teachings of Jesus Christ. Lying with intent to deceive or create a misleading impression of what the Bible did not say or a joke that is not spiritually encouraging is not a character of a disciple. Disciples of Jesus Christ are truthful to His Word because they are accountable to God, not man. These disciples run away from greed and covetousness because God has taken over their hearts. Greed for money has made some followers of Christ to compromise in so many ways to do evil things to get money or to get things done in an ungodly manner.

A deceitful heart thinks that by doing good to cover up evil, their evil will not count. God is calling you today to repent and surrender your heart to Him. Disciples guard their heart with the Word of God to secure it from evil thought. Matthew 15:19–20 (NLT) says: "For from the heart come evil thoughts, murder, adultery, all sexual immorality, theft, lying, and slander. These are what defile you. Eating with unwashed hands will never defile you."

God looks at the inside, not the outside. Unwashed hands or human doctrines cannot defile a person according to Jesus Christ because it is a tradition of men. The doctrine and tradition of believers in Jesus Christ is the Word of God. The pressure of culture or godless ideas should not be taken more seriously than the Word of God.

Jesus Christ's message for the church is that His Word should be emphasized and taken seriously more than manmade rules and ideas. Sin and godless ideas can actually defile a man. The heart is where thought and intentions, whether good or evil, come from. Luke 6:45 (NLT) says: "A good person produces good things from the treasury of a good heart, and an evil person produces evil things from the treasury of an evil heart. What you say flows from what is in your heart."

Disciples operate with the mind of Christ by taking a decision to follow Jesus Christ and do what is right. These disciples worship God wholeheartedly. It's not just lip service. God takes over the heart of His disciples by replacing their old heart with a new one. What defiles a man flows from what is in the heart because any heart that has not truly surrendered and remains loyal to God is deceitful and wicked. God has the power to change any heart that confesses and repents from sin and evil. Disciples always guard their heart with the Word of God to resist the devil when he comes with his schemes, lies, and deceptions.

Disciples use the Word of God skillfully as their weapon against the schemes of the devil. They are truthful, genuine, and transparent before God and to one another. Jesus Christ commissions His disciples to go and make disciples with sincerity of heart. This Great Commission is applicable to the living church of God today, to proclaim the gospel with a prophetic voice that is loud and clear about salvation and repentance from sins. God has given these disciples the power to proclaim the Word with boldness, not because of superiority or self-righteous, but to win souls to God's kingdom. Matthew 28:18–20 (NLT) says:

"Jesus came and told his disciples, "I have been given all authority in heaven and on earth. Therefore, go and make disciples of all the nations, baptizing them in the name of the Father and the Son and the Holy Spirit. Teach these new disciples to obey all the commands I have given you. And be sure of this: I am with you always, even to the end of the age."

2.4 LAMP

As a lamp is the source of light that extinguishes darkness, so the Word of God is the lamp that provides light for Christians not to walk in the path of darkness. Living in godliness is walking in the path of light by the guidance of the Word of God. Psalms 119:105 (NLT) says: "Your word is a lamp to guide my feet and a light for my path."

The Word of God is the lamp that produces light for proper visibility for Christians to lead and guide them from stumbling. God's

Word helps His children to navigate through this life; it leads and guides them in every path of life. Reading the Word of God daily guides Christians to be focused so they do not stray from the right path, which is for Christians to study and practice God's Word. The lamp gives light and insight, clarifying how a Christian should live.

Not reading the Word of God can lead to spiritual blindness. The lamp is a spiritual illumination that shines God's glory in the life of a Christian who truly studies the Word and lives it. People can perceive and see something unique in the lives of Christians living in godliness. What makes these people distinct is that they are graceful by the presence of God in their life through His Word. These Christians—specifically their behavior and lifestyle—are genuine and consistent.

Living in godliness is a lifestyle that is genuinely consistent with His Word, the lamp that produces the light of God. Living in godliness is truthfulness and doing good deeds to bring praise and glory to God the Father when motives are pure. The lifestyle of truthfulness and good deeds radiate the presence of God in the life of Christians to shine as a light in this dark world. Living in godliness is the lamp that produces the light in the life of Christians to reflect the light of God because He is light. 1 John 1:5–6 (NLT) says: "This is the message we heard from Jesus and now declare to you: God is light, and there is no darkness in him at all. So we are lying if we say we have fellowship with God but go on living in spiritual darkness; we are not practicing the truth."

Godliness is having a personal relationship and fellowship with God on a daily basis and living out the truth. God desires His church to represent His kingdom as the lamp that shines out His light to speak His Word with truth and boldness. The church of the living God is to shine as a light in every part of the world by the way Christians live and speak. Christians are admonished not to compromise God's Word but to stand out in the way they live among the ungodly so that the uniqueness in the life of a Christian can be clearly seen. Matthew 5:14–16 (NLT) says:

> You are the light of the world—like a city on a hilltop that cannot be hidden. No one lights a lamp and then puts it under a basket. Instead, a lamp is placed on a stand, where it gives light to everyone in the house. In the same way, let your good deeds shine out for all to see, so that everyone will praise your heavenly Father.

The lamp is the essence of the Word of God, which transforms the heart of a Christian to reflect Christ and live by example. The inner transformation of what God has done in the life of a Christian leads to living in godliness. The Word of God is the lamp that illuminates ways of the godly to live a righteous and a godly life in Christ Jesus. The oil in the lamp, which is the Holy Spirit, helps a Christian to gain knowledge and walk in the ways of God to live as children of light to the world.

Healthy eyes see His Word the way God sees it. The healthy eyes are spiritual eyes that are developed by reading the Word of God daily through the power of the Holy Spirit to guide God's children to see beyond the physical. Spiritual darkness cannot overshadow spiritual illumination because His Word has the power to extinguish darkness. Jesus Christ is the only source that has the power to light up the lamp of Christians who put their trust and abide in Him. John 12:44–46 (NLT) says:

> "Jesus shouted to the crowds, "If you trust me, you are trusting not only me, but also God who sent me. For when you see me, you are seeing the one who sent me. I have come as a light to shine in this dark world, so that all who put their trust in me will no longer remain in the dark."

Christians should desire to walk in the light of God daily by exercising godliness. Exercising godliness enables Christians to gain divine understanding and to develop good judgment as they read the Word of God. Unhealthy eyes cannot see clearly into God's Word to give sound judgment because the spiritual eyes are blind to the truth.

The Word of God is the light that shines in the life of a Christian to shape him or her in the way to live. Healthy eyes are developed when Christians make a deliberate choice and effort with their eyes of what to read or see. The kinds of things that appeal to Christians with their eyes depends on if they have healthy or unhealthy eyes.

What Christians read or see speaks volumes and will determine if their bodies are full of light or darkness. Healthy eyes look at what is holy and pure in the sight of God. Luke 11:34-36 (NIV) says: "Your eye is the lamp of your body. When your eyes are healthy, your whole body also is full of light. But when they are unhealthy, your body also is full of darkness. See to it then that the light within you is not darkness. Therefore, if your whole body is full of light, and no part of it dark, it will be just as full of light as when a lamp shines its light on you."

Godliness is walking and living out God's Word, the full light that shines out in the life of Christian to make a difference. Christian life radiates the presence and glory of God because of the light of God. The godly are spiritually alert, vigilant, and very watchful for their lamp not to be dim in the way they live and use their eyes. God's Word helps these Christians to develop spiritual eyes in such a way to recognize what is not godly with help of the Holy Spirit to resist evil. When the lamp is dim, the Christian struggles spiritually not to see things the way God perceive things.

Living in godliness is walking in the light of God in preparedness for the coming of the Lord Jesus Christ. The race is worth running because the coming of the Lord is eminent. These Christians have made Christ their focus, and living wisely and not going against

God's Word is at the center of their lives. They are waiting and preparing for the coming of the Lord not to take them unawares. The lamp guides the godly to watch with their light on to guide and lead in every path of their life to please God. 1 Thessalonians 5:1–10 (NLT) says:

> "Now concerning how and when all this will happen, dear brothers and sisters, we don't really need to write you. For you know quite well that the day of the Lord's return will come unexpectedly, like a thief in the night. When people are saying, "Everything is peaceful and secure," then disaster will fall on them as suddenly as a pregnant woman's labor pains begin. And there will be no escape. But you aren't in the dark about these things, dear brothers and sisters, and you won't be surprised when the day of the Lord comes like a thief. For you are all children of the light and of the day; we don't belong to darkness and night. So be on your guard, not asleep like the others. Stay alert and be clearheaded. Night is the time when people sleep and drinkers get drunk. But let us who live in the light be clearheaded, protected by the armor of faith and love, and wearing as our helmet the confidence of our salvation. For God chose to save us through our Lord Jesus Christ, not to pour out his anger on us. Christ died for us so that, whether we are dead or alive when he returns, we can live with him forever."

Living in godliness is living in the light of God to love others as a follower of Christ. Christians who do not know how to love or love only those they can relate with are blinded by the darkness. Loving fellow believers is living in the light of God. When Christians pretend to love to cover up their hatred, it is misleading and can cause others to stumble. Christians who claim to be in the light and hate a fellow believer are very deceptive and still operate in darkness. The

Word of God teaches and guides Christians to love genuinely as the evidence of living in godliness. 1 John 2:9–11 (NLT) says:

> "If anyone claims, "I am living in the light," but hates a fellow believer, that person is still living in darkness. Anyone who loves a fellow believer is living in the light and does not cause others to stumble. But anyone who hates a fellow believer is still living and walking in darkness. Such a person does not know the way to go, having been blinded by the darkness."

2.5 INTEGRITY

Integrity means honesty, not compromising the Word of God, and using the Bible as the standard of living. Godliness is a spiritual exercise that promotes integrity and dictates how a Christian should live. Integrity for the godly is so important because it shows how much the Word of God has really transformed them from the inside. The godly enthrone God in their lives by reflecting the wholesome teaching of the Word of God in what they do and how they live. Living in godliness is a lifestyle of integrity for Christians to give it all to God Almighty. Their ways are honest because they are practical Christians who practice His Word and live by it. It is difficult to live a godly life without living an honest lifestyle. God protects and defends Christians who walk in integrity.

Proverbs 2:7 (NLT) says: "He grants a treasure of common sense to the honest. He is a shield to those who walk with integrity." God is a shield to those who walk with integrity. Integrity as a child of God matters so much for the church of the living God because it is about truthfulness. The lifestyle of truthfulness and honesty goes together, and it pleases God. That is why God grants a treasure of common sense to Christians who live in godliness. These Christians live by example of what the Bible requires of the church. Titus 2:7–8 (NLT) says:

"And you yourself must be an example to them by doing good works of every kind. Let everything you do reflect the integrity and seriousness of your teaching. Teach the truth so that your teaching can't be criticized. Then those who oppose us will be ashamed and have nothing bad to say about us."

Living in godliness is doing good works in everything that reflects and represents the integrity of the gospel of Christ. Living in godliness is a reflection of the integrity and seriousness of the teaching of Jesus Christ about God's kingdom. His teachings should reflect blameless and godly lifestyles. Jesus Christ was known for His honesty and truthfulness during His ministry. God expects that kind of lifestyle from every believer because that was the reason Jesus Christ came through Him.

God's people can live in godliness. By His example in the way He lived, Jesus Christ showed the church the way to live in an upright manner. That was why Jesus shed His blood to cleanse us from sin and all unrighteousness to make a distinct difference in the way we live. Practicing to live like Jesus Christ is a life of integrity and truthfulness. Matthew 22:16 (NLT) says: "They sent some of their disciples, along with the supporters of Herod, to meet with him. 'Teacher,' they said, 'we know how honest you are. You teach the way of God truthfully. You are impartial and don't play favorites."

The Pharisees observed honesty in the life of Jesus Christ in the way He taught God's truth to the people. Living in godliness is a life of impartiality and speaking the truth at all times without playing favorites. Living in godliness is a consistent behavior that aligns with biblical doctrines of God's Word. With these Christians, their integrity comes from knowing God with a genuine heart because they follow the example of Jesus Christ.

God desires His church to be honest and trustworthy. Christ followers who are honest in their faith in God Almighty have holy reverence for God. God's people are those who fear Him and hate evil. According to the Bible, Jethro advised Moses to select the God-fearing people, those who are truthful and honest, for a leadership position. Exodus 18:21 (NLT) says: "But select from all the people some capable, honest men who fear God and hate bribes. Appoint them as leaders over groups of one thousand, one hundred, fifty, and ten."

Honesty and devotion is a lifestyle of sincerity of living in godliness before God Almighty and toward all believers. Devotion to the work of God should be done with right motives for the edification of the body of Christ and to the glory of God. According to 1 Thessalonians 2:10 (NLT) says: "You yourselves are our witnesses—and so is God—that we were devout and honest and faultless toward all of you believers."

2.6 NEWS

This news is good news because it is from a reliable source. It is about the salvation that God offered to humanity through Jesus Christ. That is why this news is trustworthy and reliable. The Holy Bible, the inspired Word of God, is the only means of conveying this important information to the world. The Bible gives clear information about things that everyone needs to know—information about past and current events and what will happen in the future. This news stands the test of times because it is from a reliable source.

God has the power to set free anyone who believes in this good news. Jesus Christ declares and proclaims these words for the liberation of humanity. Isaiah 61:1 (NLT) says: "The Spirit of the Sovereign Lord is upon me, for the Lord has anointed me to bring good news to the poor. He has sent me to comfort the brokenhearted and to proclaim that captives will be released and prisoners will be freed."

This news is about freedom and liberation for the oppressed. People must desire to be set free by God to enable them to live in godliness. This news is all about His Royal Majesty, King Jesus Christ, the Deliverer of the World, who came to destroy the work of the devil. This news about King Jesus is preeminent because He has no rival and no equal in His superiority. The good news is that King Jesus died for all to be saved because He is supreme. This great news is about how God purchased the freedom of humanity with a high price, the blood of His Son Jesus Christ, the King of all Kings. Jesus Christ shed His precious blood for the remission of our sins to pay for our freedom to enable His children to live in godliness. These freedoms also include our liberation from bondage, captivity, oppression, and the stronghold of sin under the powers of Satan. This good news empowers God's people to live in this freedom, a lifestyle of godliness.

The greatest gift and miracle that God gave to humanity is the good news of salvation. The news is the power of the salvation of God because God demonstrated His love, mercy, kindness, and grace to all humanity through the cross. The news is that everyone willing to receive the offer can be saved. Obedience to this good news is what is required of those who accept and believe the news; the reward is eternal life. The only credential needed is to belief in what Jesus Christ has done on the cross and an acceptance of Him. Only the blood of Jesus Christ can wash away sins and break bondages. That is why the good news is vital and powerful.

Deliverance from bondage and captivity comes only from the power that is in the good news if you believe the Word of God. Acts 2:38 (NLT) says: "Peter replied, 'Each of you must repent of your sins and turn to God, and be baptized in the name of Jesus Christ for the forgiveness of your sins. Then you will receive the gift of the Holy Spirit.'"

The news of the salvation is about repentance and forgiveness, asking God for His mercy, no matter what you have done in the past. He is inviting you to come to Him. Jesus Christ wants you to come and reason with you and make you a new person. Isaiah 1:18 (KJV) says: "Come now, and let us reason together, saith the Lord: though your sins be as scarlet, they shall be as white as snow; though they are red like crimson, they shall be as wool."

Eternal life is the ultimate goal that you will ever need in life by accepting this good news because the wages of sin is death, everlasting separation from God in hellfire. Any news that pretends to be the good news of the Lord Jesus Christ does not have the power to save and deliver because it is counterfeited and is not reliable. The counterfeit news is misleading people to the wrong direction because some part of the good news is omitted.

The church of God should focus constantly on the good news as a reminder of what Jesus Christ did on the cross to free humanity so people will genuinely repent from sin and evil. Faith without repentance is not the good news because it is a false hope. Faith in Jesus Christ is to believe and accept the offer of the good news to repent.

Godly repentance breaks the power of sin and the oppression of Satan. Some Christians have turned away from the truth because they have been fooled by those who deliberately twist the truth about the good news of salvation. Galatians 1:6–7 (NLT) says:

"I am shocked that you are turning away so soon from God, who called you to himself through the loving mercy of Christ. You are following a different way that pretends to be the Good News but is not the Good News at all. You are being fooled by those who deliberately twist the truth concerning Christ."

Living in godliness is seeking the kingdom of God in sincerity through Jesus Christ so that bondages and the powers of sin to be broken by God's power alone. The good news has the power to transform life and bring changes in the life of any individual. The story of Jesus Christ is the only valuable and important news that opens the door of redemption to humanity. This news is worth listening to and hearing because it has the power to change life. This news is all about the person of Jesus Christ the Savior, who brought good news of salvation to the world.

The news is that, when you believe, you must repent from your sins to receive forgiveness. This news is not like any kind of news. The news about Jesus is very important news to all humanity because only through Jesus Christ can people be saved. The invitation to receive the good news is open to all and is free. God made this news available to all humanity so there would be no excuses. This good news also includes our debts of sins that were paid off on the cross by God Almighty.

Sins are eliminated because the cleansing power of the blood of Jesus Christ washes them away. All you have to do to repent from your sins is to accept Christ into your lives. Jesus Christ declares that He is the only and one way to God the Father, the Creator of the world. There's no other way. God Almighty, the Creator of the universe, does not recognize any other way. Jesus Christ is the only source of a genuine salvation, truth, and hope for humanity. Any other source is nothing but a false hope and deception. Jesus Christ is the only source of the bread of life and living water that nourishes the body, mind, and soul. He is the source of the living water that flows within an individual as soon as he or she receives Christ genuinely into his or her life.

God totally transforms any person who encounters Christ for real through the power of the Holy Spirit forever. This experience is a life-changer because it is in the good news that a person can experience joy, love, peace, and hope to live in godliness. Matthew 4:17 (NLT) says: "From then on Jesus began to preach, 'Repent of your sins and turn to God, for the Kingdom of Heaven is near.'"

The news is that the kingdom of heaven can be experienced when a person genuinely repents from sins. It leads to living in godliness. The news in the message of Jesus Christ to everyone is to repent from sins and turn to God for the individual to experience the kingdom of heaven while on earth here, waiting for the coming of the Lord to take His church with Him to His perfect kingdom, which is the kingdom of God. In the kingdom of heaven, only the will of God operates. The atmosphere of love with the presence of God rules there. That is why living in godliness for Christians on earth is a glimpse of what is going on in the kingdom of heaven. The Bible says to let the will of God be done on earth here as it is done in heaven. Matthew 6:10 (KJV) says: "Thy kingdom come. Thy will be done in earth as it is in heaven."

The church is encouraged to continue to work with the love of God and one purpose, to teach and preach the good news, which is the core message to live in God's righteousness. The good news has the power to rescue because the coverage of God's protection is total for life. Godliness is a lifestyle that is consistent with genuine repentance, which is the foundation of a Christian walk with God. The good news comes with eternal joy, peace, and God's love. The gifts of the Holy Spirit come with the salvation of souls. This is the kind of unspeakable joy that drives the godly to preach the good news without wrong motives for people to be saved. God is interested for souls to be saved by turning away from your sins and embracing Him. The news is that everyone is invited to receive the gift of salvation that Jesus Christ offers to all. The choice is in your hands. Isaiah 55:1–2 (NLT) says:

> "Is anyone thirsty? Come and drink—even if you have no money! Come, take your choice of wine or milk—it's all free! Why spend your money on food that does not give you strength? Why pay for food that does you no good? Listen to me, and you will eat what is good. You will enjoy the finest food".

This good news comes with everything you need in life when you seek the kingdom of God first. Money, fame, wealth, or status cannot buy this salvation. The news is that salvation is the seal for the godly as a helmet of God's protection. Accepting Jesus Christ alone into your life by repenting from your sins is what is required of you because no one can earn the salvation of God. Jesus Christ earned it on the cross for humanity. It is a gift from God Almighty for you to receive. John 4:10–14 (NLT) says:

> "Jesus replied, "If you only knew the gift God has for you and who you are speaking to, you would ask me, and I would give you living water." "But sir, you don't have a rope or a bucket," she said, "and this well is very deep. Where would you get this living water? And besides, do you think you're greater than our ancestor Jacob, who gave us this well? How can you offer better water than he and his sons and his animals enjoyed?" Jesus replied, "Anyone who drinks this water will soon become thirsty again. But those who drink the water I give will never be thirsty again. It becomes a fresh, bubbling spring within them, giving them eternal life."

The dialogue between Jesus Christ and the woman of Samaria by the well changes her for life because she accepted the gift to drink from the living water Jesus offered to her. This woman sincerely encounters Jesus Christ and empties herself before Him, and the Lord fills her with joy. The woman accepts the news that changes her perception forever. She experiences the fresh, bubbling spring water, which is the power of the Holy Spirit that works within the godly for this life here and to eternity. The experience of the living water transforms and changes lives to enable Christians to live in godliness. The Holy Spirit helps Christians to distinguish between evil and good.

Without the inner transformation, it will be very difficult to live a godly lifestyle. The inner transformation to live in godliness must involve your heart, soul, and mind. The living water is the power of God that flows in the life of His people, which is the presence of God. It is the power of the Holy Spirit that works within the godly and nourishes them daily to worship God in truth and spirit. The news reveals the truth about God and His kingdom. John 4:24 (KJV) says that Jesus told the woman by the well, "God is a Spirit: and they that worship Him must worship Him in spirit and in truth."

God is ready to pour out or rekindle His Spirit upon any person who desires to be filled. You just have to be willing to rid your life of every form of ungodliness and surrender to Jesus Christ. The good news is the love and grace of God, demonstrated in the person of Jesus Christ sent by God to save everyone who believes. It is absolutely the grace of God that can make it possible to live a new life in Christ. That is why the news also reveals the consequences of the choices people make. Refusing to repent and living in an ungodly manner and rejecting Jesus Christ will be a life of regret and pain forever. Human philosophy cannot compromise God's standard.

The biblical truth is that the Bible is the only source that is reliable and dependable for God's people as the source of reference. It is very dangerous to use any person, not even false teachers and preachers, as a source of reference. The lives you live on earth determine where you will spend your eternity. Any teachings that are not aligning with the biblical truth are lies to mislead and deceive people for destruction. Apostle Peter addressed the church long a time, and again it is applicable to the church of today. 2 Peter 2:12–22 (NLT) says:

"These false teachers are like unthinking animals, creatures of instinct, born to be caught and destroyed. They scoff at things they do not understand, and like animals, they will be destroyed. Their destruction is their reward for the harm they have done. They love to indulge in evil pleasures in broad daylight. They are a disgrace and a stain among you. They delight in deception even as they eat with you in your fellowship meals. They commit adultery with their eyes, and their desire for sin is never satisfied. They lure unstable people into sin, and they are well trained in greed. They live under God's curse. They have wandered off the right road and followed the footsteps of Balaam son of Beor, who loved to earn money by doing wrong. But Balaam was stopped from his mad course when his donkey rebuked him with a human voice. These people are as useless as dried-up springs or as mist blown away by the wind. They are doomed to blackest darkness. They brag about themselves with empty, foolish boasting. With an appeal to twisted sexual desires, they lure back into sin those who have barely escaped from a lifestyle of deception. **They promise freedom, but they themselves are slaves of sin and corruption**. For you are a slave to whatever controls you. And when people escape from the wickedness of the world by knowing our Lord and Savior Jesus Christ and then get tangled up and enslaved by sin again, they are worse off than before. It would be better if they had never known the way to righteousness than to know it and then reject the command they were given to live a holy life. They prove the truth of this proverb: "A dog returns to its vomit." And another says, "A washed pig returns to the mud."

PONDER ON THESE WORDS

The news is how God demonstrated His amazing love for all humanity. This good news is all about the salvation that God offers to the world through Jesus Christ for the remission of our sins. Recognize that you are a sinner, humble yourself, come to God with a heart of repentance from your sins, and ask for God's mercy upon your life. That is what is required. God is willing to forgive and make you a new person to experience living in godliness. Only the blood of Jesus Christ can wash away sins and provide safety. Eternal life is real, the ultimate goal that you can ever receive. Accepting Jesus Christ as the Lord and Savior of your life is a miracle and only gift that you will ever need to live in godliness. Jesus Christ is inviting you today, if you have not yet accepted Him into your life as your Lord and personal Savior. Or as a Christian, if you have drifted away from the truth, please come and make a new commitment to Him in your heart because God loves you so much.

2.7 ENCOURAGE

God encourages and inspires His children through His Word or speaks directly on a daily basis to correct and discipline His children. That is why followers of Jesus Christ are encouraged and inspired by God through sound biblical teachings to sharpen one another with the biblical truth in their walk with God. Apostle Paul encouraged the followers of the church in Corinth, which is comparable to the church of today, not be tired in the work God has called them to do because their labor is not going to be in vain. He admonishes the church to be strong and immovable in doing the work of God.

Encouragement from the Word of God drives Christians with passion and zeal with much energy for the work of God to live in godliness. 1 Corinthians 15:58 (NLT) says: "So, my dear brothers and my sisters, be strong and immovable. Always work enthusiastically for the Lord, for you know that nothing you do for the Lord is ever useless."

Christians are encouraged that every work that is done for the sake of the kingdom of God is not useless. Living in godliness is doing the work of God even if nobody is seeing you. Doing the work of God is not for self-gratification or the recognition of men because it is the right thing to do for God's kingdom. Without biblical truth, Christians cannot be encouraged and inspired to grow in the knowledge of the Word of God. Encouragements from His Word inspire

Christians to grow and develop spiritually. His Word disciplined Christians to have intimacy with God in their daily walk with God. Hebrews 12:5–13 (NLT) says:

> "And have you forgotten the encouraging words God spoke to you as his children? He said, "My child, don't make light of the Lord's discipline, and don't give up when he corrects you. For the Lord disciplines those he loves, and he punishes each one he accepts as his child." As you endure this divine discipline, remember that God is treating you as his own children. Who ever heard of a child who is never disciplined by its father? If God doesn't discipline you as he does all of his children, it means that you are illegitimate and are not really his children at all. Since we respected our earthly fathers who disciplined us, shouldn't we submit even more to the discipline of the Father of our spirits, and live forever? For our earthly fathers disciplined us for a few years, doing the best they knew how. But God's discipline is always good for us, so that we might share in his holiness. No discipline is enjoyable while it is happening—it's painful! But afterward there will be a peaceful harvest of right living for those who are trained in this way. So take a new grip with your tired hands and strengthen your weak knees. Mark out a straight path for your feet so that those who are weak and lame will not fall but become strong".

Divine disciplines are a part of a Christian life to shape and mold a Christian to live in godliness. Discipline is one of the ways that God corrects His children to bring order to His church. The Word of God is also the major source of encouragement that God gave to help His church to live a disciplined life and gain spiritual wisdom. Any Christian who refuses to be disciplined by His Word cannot live a godly life.

God uses any form of discipline to correct and encourage any of His children who walk contrary to His Word. It is very heartening because God loves His children so much to warn His people the danger of living in an ungodly and unholy manner. Discipline from the Word of God helps His children to live holy and godly lives. Discipline can be so painful at times, but it is good because it teaches God's people how to live in godliness. The evidence of living a disciplined life through the Word of God is obvious in the lifestyle of a Christian. Christians who refuse to walk in God's way cannot be living a disciplined life to please Him. Any child who refuses to be disciplined by his or her parents can never learn and become a better person.

As our relationships with our earthly parents are very important to correct and teach us to be better children, so our relationship with God is also very significant. When Christians use His Word to discipline their lives, the result is that generations will be influenced. The Word of God encourages Christians through their lifestyle to add value to the society. Living in godliness is a pathway to life for Christians who accept for God's Word to discipline them. Proverbs 10:17 (NLT) says: "People who accept discipline are on the pathway to life, but those who ignore correction will go astray."

2.8 SOLDIERS

Soldiers of Christ are Christians who are in God's army, and the captain of the army is the Lord Jesus Christ, the commander-in-chief. Isaiah 51:15 (NLT) says: "For I am the LORD your God, who stirs up the sea, causing its waves to roar. My name is the LORD of Heaven's Armies."

Soldiers of Christ are Christians who are trained and equipped with God's Word to be bold, faithful, loyal, and disciplined to work in the fullness of Christ. They live and exercise godliness attributes. These devoted Christians are committed to the Lord of heaven's army and are ready to serve in the vineyard of God with all sincerity. They are armed with spiritual armor, which is the Word of God, to fight every battle with the help of the Holy Spirit.

The Word of God is the spiritual weapon that God has given to His soldiers to defeat Satan and his agents. Soldiers of Christ are not double-minded, but they are diligent and equipped with God's Word to fight the enemy. Living in godliness is a lifestyle of soldiers of Christ. They are determined and courageous, with the help of Holy Spirit, to fight the good fight of faith to win. They rely completely on the strength of God, the Lord of Heaven's Armies, to face any battle because they are committed to God at all times. They use the Word of God as their weapon against all strategies of the enemy.

The Word of God daily disciplines and prepares soldiers of Christ to live a godly lifestyle. They listen to the voice of God before taking any decision to embark on anything, in accordance with the Word of God. They are spiritually alert and vigilantly guided with the belt of truth and godliness. They are passionate about things that matter most to God. They carry out the mission of God, not theirs. These are genuine Christians who have totally surrendered all to God's leadership alone by the leading of the Holy Spirit. They are spiritually and heavenly minded, selfless to serve with all their heart because their ultimate aim is to do the will of God.

God has trained them to skillfully use the Word of God to face any battle and win. Psalms 18:34–35 (NLT) says: "He trains my hands for battle; he strengthens my arm to draw a bronze bow. You have given me your shield of victory. Your right hand supports me; your help has made me great." Soldiers of Christ are disciplined and always on guard, and they never give up. Focused and determined, they are not distracted from His Word.

The Lord gave me a scenario of soldiers in a particular country. These soldiers undergo training before they are sent to the battlefield. They are trained to be disciplined and very focused in their mission and their goal, and they are not distracted. They have been trained to recognize the voice of their leader and remain very sensitive in their surroundings. These soldiers take instructions and commands from their commander-in-chief to follow directions.

But when a soldier fails to listen to the instructions and follow directions, he or she walks into danger without knowing. He or she finds himself or herself in the camp of his or her enemy, either because he or she was distracted or disobedient or he or she wanted to do it in his or her own way without following guidelines.

Such soldiers who fail to take orders or listen to instructions fall into the trap of the enemy unknowingly without realizing the immediate implications. Sometimes such soldiers get wounded before being rescued or even killed in the hands of the enemy unless a stronger commander-in-chief reinforces and intervenes. That is why anyone who desires to be in the military as a soldier in a country must be prepared to learn the rules before going into any battle. Soldiers who want to please their officers do not get tied up in the affairs of civilian life. Apostle Paul gave these instructions to Timothy as a soldier of Christ, which is very relevant to the church of the living God today. According to 2 Timothy 2:1–5 (NLT) says:

> "Timothy, my dear son, be strong through the grace that God gives you in Christ Jesus. You have heard me teach things that have been confirmed by many reliable witnesses. Now teach these truths to other trustworthy people who will be able to pass them on to others. Endure suffering along with me, as a good soldier of Christ Jesus. Soldiers don't get tied up in the affairs of civilian life, for then they cannot please the officer who enlisted them. And athletes cannot win the prize unless they follow the rules."

Living in godliness as a soldier of Christ is a lifestyle of orderliness and discipline. Endurance and perseverance must be exercised as a soldier of Christ to confront any battle or trial. Christians must realize that every redeemed child of God faces spiritual battles in different ways. That is why Christians must be fervent in prayer and have the knowledge of God's Word, the guideline for Christians to live in godliness.

Living in godliness is a threat to the kingdom of darkness. That is why believers face persecution and spiritual battles. Spiritual battles are not against flesh-and-blood enemies. According to Ephesians 6:10–18 (NLT) says:

"A final word: Be strong in the Lord and in his mighty power. Put on all of God's armor so that you will be able to stand firm against all strategies of the devil. For we are not fighting against flesh-and-blood enemies, but against evil rulers and authorities of the unseen world, against mighty powers in this dark world, and against evil spirits in the heavenly places. Therefore, put on every piece of God's armor so you will be able to resist the enemy in the time of evil. Then after the battle you will still be standing firm. Stand your ground, putting on the belt of truth and the body armor of God's righteousness. For shoes, put on the peace that comes from the Good News so that you will be fully prepared. In addition to all of these, hold up the shield of faith to stop the fiery arrows of the devil. Put on salvation as your helmet, and take the sword of the Spirit, which is the word of God. Pray in the Spirit at all times and on every occasion. Stay alert and be persistent in your prayers for all believers everywhere."

Soldiers of Christ are conquerors through Christ because they are persistent through prayer with the shield of faith to stop the fiery arrows of the devil. God takes care of every battle of a Christian who walks in godliness, "Nay, in all these things, we are more than conquerors through him who loved us" Romans 8:37 (KJV).

One of the ways to hear from God is through His Word so we can know His will in every situation. The godly have the determination to study the Word of God to obey the instructions of the Lord. Soldiers of Christ continuously follow God's standard because they are steadfast and faithful to the teachings of Christ. Sin and disobedience results in disconnection from God, if not repented from. Deliberate disobedience to the Word of God is ungodly and undisciplined. Soldiers of Christ hear the voice of God and follow His instructions to exercise godliness. Soldiers of Christ are representatives of Jesus Christ to do God's will as He directs them. John 7:16–18 (NLT) says:

> "So Jesus told them, "My message is not my own; it comes from God who sent me. Anyone who wants to do the will of God will know whether my teaching is from God or is merely my own. Those who speak for themselves want glory only for themselves, but a person who seeks to honor the one who sent him speaks truth, not lies."

God's mission is that of the soldiers of Christ. To live in godliness, total attention must not be given to anyone else but to God Almighty alone. God deserves all the honor and glory when a battle is fought and won because, without the help of God, effort is fruitless. Living in godliness as believers in Jesus Christ requires us to talk about the Almighty God rather than about ourselves. Christians place God above any other in their ministry and mission. When King David and his troops defeated the Philistines, he acknowledged God and said, "God did it." 1 Chronicles 14:9–17 (NLT) says:

> "The Philistines arrived and made a raid in the valley of Rephaim. **So David asked God, "Should I go out to fight the Philistines? Will you hand them over to me?" The**

LORD replied, **"Yes, go ahead. I will hand them over to you."** So David and his troops went up to Baal-perazim and defeated the Philistines there. "God did it!" David exclaimed. "He used me to burst through my enemies like a raging flood!" So they named that place Baal-perazim (which means "the Lord who bursts through"). The Philistines had abandoned their gods there, so David gave orders to burn them. But after a while the Philistines returned and raided the valley again. **And once again David asked God what to do.** "Do not attack them straight on," **God replied. "Instead, circle around behind and attack them near the poplar trees.** When you hear a sound like marching feet in the tops of the poplar trees, go out and attack! That will be the signal that God is moving ahead of you to strike down the Philistine army." **So David did what God commanded, and they struck down the Philistine army all the way from Gibeon to Gezer.** So David's fame spread everywhere, and the LORD caused all the nations to fear David."

Soldiers of Christ must exercise obedience and loyalty to do the work of God in His vineyard. God used King David mightily because he had the heart of a servant to work for God. King David knew the importance of consulting God before he embarked on that journey to attack the Philistine army. He realized that without consulting God he would not succeed.

The arm of flesh would fail any Christian who depends and relies on his or her ability to get things done without consulting God or waiting for His approval. God's power is not limited to any battle or circumstances. Christians should learn how to trust God at all times by taking their concerns and worries to God for directions to take the right step. The Word of God is the manual for Christians to find clear instructions and directives from God. It will be difficult for a Christian to fight any battle without the foundation of His Word.

The godly do not embark on any mission without clarification from God.

Without clarification from God and with willful disobedience to the instructions of God, a Christian can fall into the trap of the enemy. Compromising with your faith as a Christian is very danger-ous because that is what the devil capitalizes on. Living in godliness is walking with God in obedience and abiding under the biblical principles of the Word of God. The godly recognize that they are on the spiritual battlefield. That is why they run from evil and sin, to be spiritually alert and vigilant. Soldiers of Christ prayerfully present every need to God and wait for His response. Faithful soldiers learn how to wait and trust God because they depend on His ability to work out things for them.

2.9 SACRIFICE

The ultimate sacrifice for all humanity was the death and resurrec-tion of Jesus Christ. Jesus Christ laid down His divinity purposely to sacrifice His life to purchase the salvation of man and the freedom of humanity. Jesus Christ did not just lay down His divinity to come to earth just for our salvation alone but also to retrieve everything that Satan stole from His Children. God placed our sins and shame on Jesus Christ, the Savior of the world, to redeem His children from sins and bondages. Without the shed blood of Jesus Christ on the cross, there is no remission of sin. In fact, it would have been impos-sible to live in godliness.

The sacrifice was not cheap because it cost the Son of God His life on the cross for the atonement of our sins. Jesus Christ was res-urrected from death victoriously over principalities and powers to free His children from sin and bondages. His blood was the atone-ment for sins; through the shedding of the blood God broke the power of sin and bondage on the cross. Romans 8:3 (NLT) says:

"The law of Moses was unable to save us because of our weakness of our sinful nature. So God did what the law could not do. He sent His own Son in a body like the bodies we sinners have. And in that body God declared an end to sin's control over us by giving His Son as a sacrifice for our sins".

Living in godliness is possible as a result of what God did by giving His Son as sacrifice for our sins to declare an end to sin. Living in godliness is a sacrificial way of life through giving up of ungodly ways for the sake of the kingdom. Giving up ungodly ways is renouncing evil and sin or relationships that are not godly. True sacrifice is a broken spirit and a repentant heart. Psalms 51:17 (NLT) says: "The sacrifice you desire is a broken spirit. You will not reject a broken and a repentant heart, O God."

Living in godliness is experienced by living a sacrificial life, repenting and surrendering all to God Almighty. The ultimate sacrifices of Jesus Christ gave every true follower of Christ the privilege to live a sacrificial life and to overcome sin. The power of the Holy Spirit is able to help any individual who is willing to renounce anything that is contrary to the Will of God. Evil must be renounced because God detests the sacrifices of the wicked. Proverbs 15:8 (NLT) says: "The Lord detests the sacrifice of the wicked, but he delights in the prayers of the upright."

The heart of worship and thanksgiving is a sacrificial lifestyle to honor God. Living in godliness is a lifestyle of determination to praise God and give thanks in worship at all times. God's sacrificial love and the great things He does for humanity are enough reasons to give Him sacrificial praise and unconditional worship. Psalms 107:21–22 (NLT) says: "Let them praise the LORD for his great love and for the wonderful things he has done for them. Let them offer sacrifices of thanksgiving and sing joyfully about his glorious acts."

Christians who deliberately continue to sin after receiving the knowledge of the truth about Christ should understand that there is no more any other sacrifices that will cover such sins. Hebrews 10:26–31 (NLT) says:

> "Dear friends, if we deliberately continue sinning after we have received knowledge of the truth, there is no longer any sacrifice that will cover these sins. There is only the terrible expectation of God's judgment and the raging fire that will consume his enemies. For anyone who refused to obey the Law of Moses was put to death without mercy on the testimony of two or three witnesses. Just think how much worse the punishment will be for those who have trampled on the Son of God, and have treated the blood of the covenant, which made us holy, as if it were common and unholy, and have insulted and disdained the Holy Spirit who brings God's mercy to us. For we know the one who said, "I will take revenge. I will pay them back." He also said, "The LORD will judge his own people." It is a terrible thing to fall into the hands of the living God."

God's Word is very loud and clear for those who still indulge in unholy and ungodly lifestyles. "The LORD will judge his own people"; if a Christian is still deliberately living a lifestyle of sin after receiving the knowledge of truth, there is no longer any other sacrifice for that individual. There is no excuse for that individual because God's sacrifice is enough to make His people live in godliness.

God desires His people to live a sacrificial lifestyle by treating the blood of Jesus Christ in high esteem in the way they live. Living in godliness is imitating God and living as children of light. In the church of the living God, there should not be any kind of sin among God's people because Christians are to live a pleasing lifestyle to honor God. Ephesians 5:1–10 (NLT) says:

"Follow God's example, therefore, as dearly loved children and walk in the way of love, just as Christ loved us and gave himself up for us as a fragrant offering and sacrifice to God. But among you there must not be even a hint of sexual immorality, or of any kind of impurity, or of greed, because these are improper for God's holy people. Nor should there be obscenity, foolish talk or coarse joking, which are out of place, but rather thanksgiving. For of this you can be sure: No immoral, impure or greedy person—such a person is an idolater—has any inheritance in the kingdom of Christ and of God. Let no one deceive you with empty words, for because of such things God's wrath comes on those who are disobedient. Therefore do not be partners with them. For you were once darkness, but now you are light in the Lord. Live as children of light (for the fruit of the light consists in all goodness, righteousness and truth) and find out what pleases the Lord."

God's Word admonished Christians to imitate God in everything they do following the example of Jesus Christ. Jesus Christ is the standard for Christians to look up to Him, not to any individual. To live in godliness, Christ must be the focus.

Christ's sacrifice on the cross is to make a difference in the life of any individual who accepts Him into his or her life. Jesus Christ sacrifices His life to carry our sins and shame upon Himself for God's people to live in holiness and godliness. Living in deception and a lifestyle of sin because of the grace of God is a lifestyle of bringing shame to the name of the Lord. God's people should not be fooled by anyone who tries to excuse the lifestyle of ungodliness or even participate in the things the ungodly do. That kind of lifestyle is unacceptable because God is displeased with such a lifestyle.

Please come back to the Lord and make a fresh commitment to Him by repenting from your sins to escape everlasting punishment. Anyone who claims to be a Christian and still lives in immorality, impurity, or greed, and generally a lifestyle of sin have no place among God's people. Romans 6:13 (NIV) says:

> "Therefore do not let sin reign in your mortal body so that you obey its evil desires. Do not offer any part of yourself to sin as an instrument of wickedness, but rather offer your-selves to God as those who have been brought from death to life: and offer every part of yourself to him as an instrument of righteousness."

Living in godliness is a lifestyle of sacrifice for those Christians who have decided and made up their minds to follow Jesus Christ at all costs. Living in godliness is a lifestyle of worship and honoring Jesus Christ in the life of God-fearing people, because they carefully determine what pleases the Lord.

CHAPTER 3

Traits of Godliness

§

WHEN CHRISTIANS TREASURE AND CHERISH the Word of God and live by it, it is a trait of godliness. God gave the church the most precious and valuable gift, His Word. God's Word is an asset to the godly and is a treasure in their hearts that merits great respect. The Word of God is the wealth of the church because it has answers and solutions to every question.

It is a trait of godliness when the hearts of people focuses on heavenly things, no matter what they have achieved, and they honor God with their resources and time. Trusting God with wealth and resources is a trait of godliness because it acknowledges God as the giver. True riches produce good works and generosity to the people in need. When a Christian is rich or wealthy and is not proud—that is a trait of godliness. 1 Timothy 6:17–19 (NLT) says:

> "Teach those who are rich in this world not to be proud and not to trust in their money, which is so unreliable. Their trust should be in God, who richly gives us all we need for our enjoyment. Tell them to use their money to do good. They should be rich in good works and generous to those in need, always being ready to share with others. By doing this they will be storing up their treasure as a good foundation for the future so that they may experience true life."

Everyone has something that he or she treasures, but God's Word surpasses them all. The godly gain wisdom and knowledge from the Word of God because it guides them in every aspect of their lives. Godliness is a pattern of lifestyle for Christians who are devoted to the Almighty God and conform to the teachings of Jesus Christ. They have distinguishing qualities that make them different from the ungodly.

The trait of godliness in an individual is the Word of God that lives in him/her that enables the individual to exhibit the character of Christ. The Holy Spirit operates inside of these Christians to produce good works. By the grace of God, sin has no power to control the godly because of the power of the Holy Spirit that lives within them. The Holy Spirit is the driving force that dwells in the life of the godly to live in godliness. Romans 8:5–12 (NLT) says:

> "Those who are dominated by the sinful nature think about sinful things, but those who are controlled by the Holy Spirit think about things that please the Spirit. So letting your sinful nature control your mind leads to death. But letting the Spirit control your mind leads to life and peace. For the sinful nature is always hostile to God. It never did obey God's laws, and it never will. That's why those who are still under the control of their sinful nature can never please God. But you are not controlled by your sinful nature. You are controlled by the Spirit if you have the Spirit of God living in you. (And remember that those who do not have the Spirit of Christ living in them do not belong to him at all.) And Christ lives within you, so even though your body will die because of sin, the Spirit gives you life because you have been made right with God. The Spirit of God, who raised Jesus from the dead, lives in you. And just as God raised Christ Jesus from the dead, he will give life to your mortal bodies by this same Spirit living within you. Therefore, dear brothers and sisters,

you have no obligation to do what your sinful nature urges you to do."

Living in godliness is living under the influence of the power of the Holy Spirit. Christians who live in godliness always rely on the power of the Holy Spirit to direct, guide, and teach. Christians who desire to live in godliness must yield to the leading of the Holy Spirit. Yielding is total surrender to God in obedience and to follow Him. Living a life that is in total control of the Holy Spirit is a trait of living in godliness. Godly people are Christ followers whose character and behavior agrees with the Word of God. These Christians preach Christ, and they live by the example of the Word of God.

3.1 BORN AGAIN

Born-again persons are those who by God's grace are regenerated, redeemed, bought, and washed with the blood of the Lamb. They have been regenerated from darkness into light. God has already forgiven them, and now they become new people in Christ Jesus. God has taken over their hearts, soul, and mind. These Christians have genuinely repented from their sins and accepted Jesus Christ to be their Lord and Savior in their lives. The Holy Spirit then takes over their lives, and God gives them the power to operate in the fullness of Christ.

Anyone who proclaims to be a Christian must be born again into the family of God to experience a new life in Christ. God's people are those who are born again into the family of God by the Holy Spirit.

Living and practicing godliness is a trait of a born-again Christian. True Christians are those who apply the Word of God daily in their lives. They have experienced a spiritual birth, which can only occur by repenting and turning away from sins and evil and to accept Jesus Christ as the Lord and personal Savior. It is impossible for a person to be born again and still continue to sin and indulge in evil deeds. 1 John 3:8–9 (NLT) says:

> "But when people keep on sinning, it shows that they belong to the devil, who has been sinning since the beginning. But the Son of God came to destroy the works of the devil. Those who have been born into God's family do not make a practice of sinning, because God's life is in them. So they can't keep on sinning, because they are children of God."

God's people flee from all evil appearances because of what Christ has done in their lives through the spiritual birth. Born-again persons have the hope of eternal life with great expectation of the return of Jesus Christ. 1 Corinthians 15:19 (KJV) says: "If in this life only we have hope in Christ, we are of all men most miserable."

The Bible makes it clear that being born again does not mean you will not face trials. Temptations and trials will come, but God already made a way of escape for His children. 2 Corinthians 4:7–10 (NLT) says:

> "But we have this treasure in jars of clay to show that this all-surpassing power is from God and not from us. We are hard pressed on every side, but not crushed; perplexed, but not in despair; persecuted, but not abandoned; struck down, but not destroyed. We always carry around in our body the death of Jesus, so that the life of Jesus may also be revealed in our body."

The joy is that, through trials and temptations, the faith of God's people is trained to endure, persevere and to overcome through God's grace. The inheritance of the Christian that endure trials is priceless. These Christians serve God with joy in the fullness of the Holy Spirit, no matter what confronts them. Their eternal joy does not depend on feelings or possession of what they have. It is the gift that comes with salvation because God has redeemed them. They are passionate and sensitive to God's Word. The secret is that they abide under the authority of God Almighty. They are spiritually and biblically sound and they do not compromise the Word of God.

The Holy Spirit lead, guide and teach them in all their ways. To experience a new life in Christ, there must be sincere broken-ness that leads to godly repentance from the heart. Godly sorrow brings repentance that changes any person for life, no matter the kind of sin or evil he or she has done in the past. The worldly sor-row brings death because, once an individual feels guilty without repentance, the result is meaningless. When sin is not confessed, one is living in bondage. Confession and repentance brings fulfill-ment and freedom in the life of a Christian to live in godliness. 2 Corinthians 7:10 (NIV) says: "Godly sorrow brings repentance that leads to salvation and leaves no regrets, but worldly sorrow brings death."

God is willing to forgive any person who comes to Him with a genuine heart of repentance. You must be born again by the Spirit of God to live a godly lifestyle. Living in godliness is a result of what Christ has done inside of you. God will give you a new heart with His Spirit to guide you to live in godliness. Spiritual birth must take place before a Christian can pursue godliness. A mind that has not be renewed, transformed, and taken over by the Holy Spirit cannot please God. Born-again persons walk according to the leading of the Holy Spirit and have the desire to live a godly lifestyle.

Participating in religious activity does not make an individual to be born again. It is a change of heart from the old ways of liv-ing to a new way in Christ. To be born again into the family of God is accepting the Lord genuinely into your life and to have a personal relationship with God. Jesus Christ gave a clear answer by revealing the truth in His own Words and said, "No one can enter the Kingdom of God without being born again." Being born again means that the old style of living in sin must give way to a new style of living in godliness. John 3:3–5 (NLT) says:

> Jesus replied, "I tell you the truth, unless you are born again, you cannot see the Kingdom of God." "What do you mean?" exclaimed Nicodemus. "How can an old man go back into his mother's womb and be born again?" Jesus replied, "I assure you, no one can enter the Kingdom of God without being born of water and the Spirit."

3.2 SELF-CONTROL

Self-control is ruling one's own life with obedience to the Holy Spirit. A Christian living in godliness always exercises self-control in everything he or she does. Without self-control, it will be very difficult to form a godly character. Without self-control, a leader cannot be successful. Righteousness and self-control go together to form a godly lifestyle. A Christian who wants to walk in the way of the Lord must be a person who is willing to surrender under the leadership of the Holy Spirit. Ephesians 4:17–31 (NLT) says:

> "With the Lord's authority I say this: Live no longer as the Gentiles do, for they are hopelessly confused. Their minds are full of darkness; they wander far from the life God gives because they have closed their minds and hardened their hearts against him. They have no sense of shame. They live for lustful pleasure and eagerly practice every kind of impurity. But that isn't what you learned about Christ. Since you have heard about Jesus and have learned the truth that comes from him, throw off your old sinful nature and your former way of life, which is corrupted by lust and deception. Instead, let the Spirit renew your thoughts and attitudes. Put on your new nature, created to be like God—truly righteous

and holy. So stop telling lies. Let us tell our neighbors the truth, for we are all parts of the same body. And "don't sin by letting anger control you." Don't let the sun go down while you are still angry, for anger gives a foothold to the devil. If you are a thief, quit stealing. Instead, use your hands for good hard work, and then give generously to others in need. Don't use foul or abusive language. Let everything you say be good and helpful, so that your words will be an encouragement to those who hear them. And do not bring sorrow to God's Holy Spirit by the way you live. Remember, he has identified you as his own, guaranteeing that you will be saved on the day of redemption. Get rid of all bitterness, rage, anger, harsh words, and slander, as well as all types of evil behavior."

A lack of self-control results in sinful actions. That is why God's Word encourages Christians to get rid of all kind of sin like bitterness, rage, anger, harsh words, slander and evil behavior. Christians are identified as followers of Christ because of their attitudes and minds that have been renewed; to become a new creature created in the image of God, truly righteous and holy. Self-control is living in a new life in Christ that leads to godliness.

3.3 CONSCIENCE

Conscience is vital in living in godliness. Godly lifestyle does not contradict the wholesome teaching. Living in godliness involves being sensitive to the Word of God. A clear conscience before God and man builds a godly lifestyle. A sensitive conscience motivates a follower of Christ to do things that are morally acceptable in the sight of God. Living in godliness is having a conscience that has good intentions and is honorable in everything a Christian is involved in. The desire of the godly is having a clear conscience and doing the things that matter most to God, which is living a pleasing lifestyle to honor Him.

The prayer of the godly is to do things with a clear conscience in accordance with His Word. Living in godliness is having a clear conscience that does not mislead others to sin. Any conscience washed with the blood of Jesus Christ has the mind of Christ. To have the mind of Christ is to do things in accordance with the Word of God, before God and all people in every aspect of life. Hebrews 13:18 (NLT) says: "Pray for us, for our conscience is clear and we want to live honorably in everything we do."

A Christian with a clear conscience will admit and take responsibility if he or she has sin to confess to God Almighty and plead for mercy. Clear consciences do not justify and encourage sin but simply admits sin that is committed before the Lord and repents. A conscience that has been cleansed by the blood of Jesus Christ is bothered anytime that Christians works against the precepts of God. 2 Samuel 24:10 (NLT) says: "But after he had taken the census, David's conscience began to bother him. And he said to the Lord, 'I have sinned greatly by taking this census. Please forgive my guilt, Lord, for doing this foolish thing."

When conscience does not conflict with God's Word, then it is pleasing to God. The godly will always release their conscience to the Holy Spirit to guide them in every step. God's people are very careful in their walk with God, and their decisions don't contradict God's Word. The conscience that has not fully surrendered to God cannot take a decision that will bring glory to God. Christians with clear consciences expose evil and wicked deeds. A worldly conscience has difficulty in understanding the things of the Spirit because it concentrates on self rather than God Almighty.

Christians who continue to live a lifestyle of sin and evil without repentance shows that they are spiritually dead. The conscience of the godly is always very sensitive in what matters most to God because the Holy Spirit leads them. If a Christian has habitual sin and is not bothered, then something is not right. This means that the individual did not truly repent at the time of his or her decision to become a Christian and that is why the conscience is not sensitive to the Holy Spirit.

The conscience cleansed with the blood of Jesus Christ understands the moral norm. The heart led by the Holy Spirit will always do the right thing to please God. A heart controlled by the Holy Spirit is filled with love for God and people. Living in godliness is having the love of God from a pure heart with a clear conscience and a genuine faith in Christ Jesus. 1 Timothy 1:5 (NLT) says: "The purpose of my instruction is that all believers would be filled with love that comes from a pure heart, a clear conscience, and genuine faith."

The corruption of minds and consciences will only produce evil. When Christians deliberately ignore the Word of God, it shows that their conscience is numb. God is able to transform and renew any heart that is willing to repent to revive its conscience. The hearts that the Holy Spirit has taken over reflects the light of God and a clear conscience.

Jesus Christ is the great high priest who offered His blood to purify our conscience when God's people sincerely seek and trust Him completely. Nothing can purify our conscience other than the blood of Jesus Christ. That is why the people of God must seek Him with a sincere heart. The blood of Jesus Christ purifies the conscience of every believer in order to have fellowship with God. Hebrews 10:21–22 (NLT) says:

"And since we have a great High Priest who rules over God's house, let us go right into the presence of God with sincere hearts fully trusting him. For our guilty consciences have been sprinkled with Christ's blood to make us clean, and our bodies have been washed with pure water."

A clear conscience lives an honorable life that brings God glory. Only the blood of Jesus Christ is superior and perfect enough to cleanse our guilty consciences to do the right thing as followers of Jesus Christ. A conscience that is free from guilt recognizes what is sin and evil in the sight of God. A clear conscience gives the godly boldness to speak the truth at all times. 1 Peter 3:16–17 (NIV) says: "Keeping a clear conscience, so that those who speak maliciously against your good behaviour in Christ may be ashamed of their slander. For it is better, if it is God's will, to suffer for doing good than to suffer for doing evil."

3.4 Forgiveness

Forgiveness is a spiritual mandate for Christians to exercise daily to live in godliness. Forgiveness is a trait in Christians who are living in godliness. Jesus Christ made it clear that for God the Father to forgive anyone, you must forgive others their wrong. God demonstrated His mercy and compassion for all humanity when none of us deserved His mercy, but He allowed His Son to die on the cross for the forgiveness of sins for all humanity. He allowed it because of His love for humanity and His mercy and kindness in forgiving our transgression through Jesus Christ who died on the cross.

For any individual who refuses to forgive, the Bible says God will not forgive that individual. Whatever you are struggling with that is holding you hostage not to forgive, Christ wants you to lay it down at His feet so that you can be set free. Forgiveness actually opens doors of blessings. Unwillingness to forgive is evil and wicked in the sight of God. God reminds His children to repent from such lifestyle and to live in godliness. Forgiveness is a spiritual obligation for all followers of Jesus Christ. Matthew 6:14-15 (NIV) says, "If you forgive other people when they sin against you, your heavenly Father will also forgive you. But if you do not forgive others their sins, your Father will not forgive your sins."

The Bible made it very clear that forgiveness is an important part of the Christian's daily lifestyle to be part of His kingdom. Forgiveness is one of the attributes of God the Father. That is why He wants His children to do likewise. The true church of Christ operates and believes in forgiveness because that is the core value for Christianity. Everyone is indebted to God Almighty for the forgiveness of sins. God immediately forgives anyone who confesses and repents from sins. The godly know that unforgiving and a bitter heart can hinder a walk with God. So they try to make peace with everyone and also forgive. Christians, if your goal is to make heaven, you must forgive anyone who wrongs you as many times as you can recall. Luke 17:1–4 (NLT) says:

> One day Jesus said to his disciples, "There will always be temptations to sin, but what sorrow awaits the person who does the tempting! It would be better to be thrown into the sea with a millstone hung around your neck than to cause one of these little ones to fall into sin. So watch yourselves! If another believer sins, rebuke that person; then if there is repentance, forgive. Even if that person wrongs you seven times a day and each time turns again and asks forgiveness, you must forgive."

Forgiveness plays a vital role for followers of Christ who want to live successful and godly lives.

3.5 Prayer
Prayer is a means of communication with God in thanksgiving, adoration, confession, and supplication. It is also an act of intercession. God has equipped His children to pray with the power of the Holy Spirit and the authority of His Word. Attitudes to prayer like unbelief and doubt and living in an ungodly lifestyle can quench the Holy

Spirit. The Holy Spirit is ready to work with the people of God when there is sincerity in their prayer lives.

Prayer will involve sacrifice of time to interact with God. It takes a step of faith to trust God unconditionally to pray—that is, praying and interceding in confidence during prayers to God. Christians meditating upon His Word are to enter the presence of God with praise, knowing fully well with assurance that He answers prayer. 1 Thessalonians 5:17–19 (KJV) says: "Pray without ceasing. In every thing give thanks: for this is the will of God concerning you. Quench not the Holy Spirit."

Prayer is a lifestyle of Christians who devote and focus their time to pray continually about everything. Prayer is very essential in the life of Christians because it is an act of worship to God Almighty. A life of prayer builds spiritual confidence that trusts God in every situation. A prayer meeting without the presence and power of God is like any other social gathering with no spiritual impact. The primary purpose of the temple of the living God is for prayer, worship, and to study the Word of God. It should be used for the activities that honor God.

Jesus Christ knew the importance of prayer because this is the heart of God for His people to pray and cry out to Him. God's Word encourages His children to cry out to Him for help. God comes to the rescue of His people when they pray and cry out to Him in distress and pain. The temple is the house of God where His people gather and pour out their hearts to God the Father. Prayer lifestyle is very crucial for the believer to live in godliness because the more you pray the closer you are to God the Father. Matthew 21:12–13 (KJV) says:

And Jesus went into the temple of God, and cast out all them that sold and bought in the temple, and overthrew the tables of the moneychangers, and the seats of them that sold doves,

And said unto them, It is written, My house shall be called the house of prayer; but ye have made it a den of thieves.

The action of Jesus Christ to the money changers is a strong message to the churches that the temple of God is specifically for prayer and not for activities that does not honor the name of God. The house of God must be a place where the people of God revere God with a holy fear and to exalt His Holy name in worship and prayer. The people of God must show respect in the activities done in the house of God. They are not to carry out activities in the temple that contradict His Word as such activities do not bring glory to Him. That is why the people of God must pray in the Spirit because the Holy Spirit reveals what needs to be prayed for.

Prayer is a habit and lifestyle that requires perseverance and endurance in even the most difficult times. Faith is an action that motivates God's people to pray. In the most difficult time, faith is tested. Trials help the faith of the people of God to grow and confidently trust God unconditionally. Hebrews 11:1 (NIV) says, "Now faith is confidence in what we hope for and assurance about what we do not see."

The right attitude to prayer is trust and depending on the Lord to lead and guide. Without faith in God, prayer will be meaningless. Christians who have the habit of prayer believe and trust God completely to work out things for them. They believe in God's intervention because they know that, with God, all things are possible. They don't have alternatives to figure out things for themselves. Christians are encouraged to build one another up in their faith and to learn how to trust God and to pray in the power of the Holy Spirit. Jude 1:20 (NLT) says: "But you, dear friends, must build each other up in your most holy faith, pray in the power of the Holy Spirit."

Praying in the power of the Holy Spirit demonstrates that God is in charge and He has taken control of the prayer meeting. It is God's will that prayer should be done with a heart of preparedness to hear from God what He wants His Children to pray about. Prayer is a time set aside to talk to God Almighty by expressing feelings and burdens to Him with great expectations from God. Prayer is not just time set aside alone, but it should be a lifestyle for Christians to pray at all times. When the people of God come together in love and unity to pray, the Holy Spirit then takes over the prayer. The results are obvious to the glory of God. The Holy Spirit does reveal things that need to be addressed during prayer.

For prayer offered with a sincere heart, God will respond. Christians who spend time in prayer have a strong bond and close relationship with God the Father. God's people who spend their time in prayer hear from God because they know Him as the Father. They depend on and trust God completely to fight for them. When Christians take their petition to God, the Lord Himself takes over and fights their battle. Prayer is one of the ways for Christians to have fellowship with Him and to build a personal strong relationship with God the Father. Prayer is a lifestyle of the godly; to exercise faith daily and to seek God's direction and His approval in every situation.

Prayer offered with a sincere heart and in line with the Word of God is effective. Even when answers are delayed, the godly knows that God will respond. Living in godliness is a lifestyle of prayer not for oneself alone but for all people. These Christians pray about everything without ceasing in the power of the Holy Spirit.

Philippians 4:6 (NLT) says: "Don't worry about anything; instead pray about everything. Tell God what you need, and thank him for all he has done." God responds to and answers sincere prayers from the heart according to His Will. Prayer is like food for those who live in godliness because they rely on the power and strength of God; they do not relent or give up.

1 Timothy 2:1–2 (NIV), "I urge, then, first of all, that petitions, prayers, intercession and thanksgiving be made for all people—for kings and all those in authority, that we may live peaceful and quiet

lives in all godliness and holiness." It is a spiritual mandate that Christians should pray and intercede for all people and those who are in authority. God delights in His children who live in godliness and holiness. Prayer is an opportunity to ask God anything in His name according to His will.

God honors prayer that is offered with a sincere heart because He is interested in the affairs of His children. Christians should not only pray to God in times of need, but should let prayer be a lifestyle. Prayer is a continuous conversation with God, knowing fully that He hears His children. The godly have confidence in the faithfulness of God to answer prayers. John 14:14 (NIV) says, "You may ask me for anything in my name, and I will do it."

Obedience to the Word of God is the most powerful access to the heart of God and is the key for effective communication with God and answered prayers. Living in godliness is a lifestyle of prayers that does not contradict God's Word. God is always ready to listen when His children pray and ask Him anything according to His will. God is willing to honor their prayers because they believe and trust Him. God will never lie. Whatever He said, He will do. The key is complete faith in God Almighty to trust Him unconditionally. These Christians stand upon the Word of God to lock and unlock doors, praying according to God's will.

His Word should guide Christians on how to pray in line with God's will. The effect of the Word of God will be manifested in the church, when believers choose to exercise their faith through prayer. It gladdens the heart of a Father when He sees His children come to meet Him, to seek His counsel or guidance from Him. A father is willing to assist his child to see that the child's needs are met. A child who knows that he or she cannot figure things out for himself or herself always runs to his or her earthly parents for solution. Every time he or she is bored or in need of something, a child who thinks it is very smart to do things on his or her own ends up making mistakes and running into problems.

The attitude of a godly Christian should be like a little child. He or she should run to God at every moment and at any time to seek God's guidance and counsel through prayer in his or her various needs. The godly relax in the arms of God to pour out their hearts to Him. God responds and answers prayer from a sincere heart.

Hannah was in trouble, and she took it to God in prayer and her prayers were answered. 1 Samuel 1:20 (NIV), "So in the course of time Hannah became pregnant and gave birth to a son. She named him Samuel, saying 'because I asked the Lord for him.'"

Christians are encouraged to wait on the Lord rather than seek the alternative for there is no true alternative. Permanent solutions for prayers come from God Almighty alone. Godliness is an act of devotion to God by constantly praying, trusting, and waiting on the Lord. I encourage the followers of Jesus Christ, with the help of the Holy Spirit, not to relent in their prayers and also be vigilant and steadfast in God.

The Word of God is the only powerful tool for Christians to use as a weapon against the strategies and devices of the enemy both in the time of prayers and in daily living. The secret is that the devil fears and reveres the Word of God, as it makes the devil and his demons powerless. Satan bows before the Lord God Almighty as he hears believers in the Lord Jesus Christ speaks God's Word. Your victory is guaranteed through Christ Jesus because, for the eyes of the Lord are on those who walk in godliness. And His ears are attentive to their prayer. 1 Peter 3:11 (NIV) says: "For the eyes of the Lord are on the righteous and his ears are attentive to their prayer, but the face of the Lord is against those who do evil."

3.6 LOVE

The love of God is sacrificial and selfless because it is pure and holy. God's love is unfailing because of His mercy toward all people.

Living in godliness is a lifestyle of living out the love of God. Love is one of the traits of a Christian as a follower of Christ. The real love is the love of God that can be fully expressed in God's people through actions and the way they live with others. The love of God is the proof that God lives in the life of a Christian through the power of the Holy Spirit.

Without practicing the love of God, it will be very difficult to live in godliness. God demonstrated His love first to humanity by allowing His Son to die on the cross for the remission of sins. God loves all humanity, even when none of us deserve it. The love of God should reflect in the lifestyle of followers of Jesus Christ to make a difference. Love that is not inspired by God is selfish because it is for personal gain and self-gratification. Any love that is selfish and self-gratifying is of the world. That kind of love craves physical pleasure and pride, to achieve selfish goals and fame and to acquire material possessions in an ungodly ways.

So many have been lured away from the love of God because of what the world has offered them, forgetting that what the devil has offered is nothing but pain and restlessness. Revelation 2:4–5 (NLT) says: "But I have this complaint against you. You don't love me or each other as you did at first! Look how far you have fallen! Turn back to me and do the works you did at first. If you don't repent, I will come and remove your lampstand from its place among the churches." The church of the living God is being reminded again to go back to their first love and repent, love God genuinely and wholeheartedly. The love of God is never tainted because the real love of God comes with divine blessings and peace. 1 John 2:15–16 (NLT) says:

"Do not love this world nor the things it offers you, for when you love the world, you do not have the love of the Father in you. For the world offers only a craving for physical pleasure, a craving for everything we see, and pride in our achievements and possessions. These are not from the Father, but are from this world."

God's love demonstrated on the cross through Jesus Christ for our salvation shows the extent of what He can do as a loving Father. His love reveals to us His salvation, mercy, justice, and judgment. He told us everything we need to know about Him. God is a loving Father who is fair and just to His judgment. This loving God made it clear in His Word that He will judge evil and sin. His patience gives everyone the opportunity to repent because one day Jesus Christ is coming back as the king and judge of the world. 2 Peter 3:9 (NLT) says: "The Lord isn't really being slow about his promise, as some people think. No, he is being patient for your sake. He does not want anyone to be destroyed, buts wants everyone to repent."

God demonstrates His love for humanity through His patience for all to be saved. Sin and evil cannot be justified because God has demonstrated His love by making a way of escape for humanity through Jesus Christ. The love of God is very powerful and can draw any individual away from sin, if the fear of God is in the heart of the individual.

Humanly speaking, to live a life of godliness, the love of God must be the primary focus in one's life. Godly lifestyle is living a sacrificial life for God and to truly crucify the old self with Christ. Through Christ, the godly can exercise a righteous character and godly lifestyle. The love of God makes the difference in the life of the godly. True love of God brings obedience with total surrender to His leadership. God has the power to cleanse anyone from all unrighteousness, if the repentance is genuine and the individual is ready to surrender to His lordship. Galatians 2:20 (NLT) says: "My old self has been crucified with Christ. It is no longer I who live, but Christ lives in me. So I live in this earthly body by trusting in the Son of God, who loved me and gave himself for me."

The truth is that the trait in living in godliness is demonstrated through the love of God that disciplines Christians to love, even in a difficult situation. The true love of God is the foundation of living in godliness, to live righteously and to love other believers. Living in godliness is a profession of the love of Jesus Christ in the life of a Christian for God. The love of God renews the mind of God-fearing people. The mind that God has transformed is conformed to think, act, and love like Christ. A mind that has been taken over by the Holy Spirit works according to the will of God. A genuine repentance produces a new way of living and to love because God has the power to transform that individual to become like Him. The love for God in the heart of a Christian brings godly sorrows that produce a genuine repentance.

Christians who genuinely love God flee from every appearances of evil because they produce fruit that supports repentance. God's love is very powerful and does not change when you return to Him in genuine repentance; He forgives. He also made it clear in His Word the consequences of sin. Revelation 22:14–15 (NLT) says: "Blessed are those who wash their robes. They will be permitted to enter through the gates of the city and eat the fruit from the tree of life. Outside are the dogs—the sorcerers, sexually immoral, murderers, idol worshippers, and all who love to live a lie."

The love for God is the driving force that helps Christian to run away from sin. "Outside are the dogs" signals a strong warning to those who are still involved in any kind of sin to repent and return to God because the day of the Lord is coming. The Bible described those who are still living in ungodly lifestyle like dogs. Any form of evil will not enter His Kingdom, whether it is the sorcerers, sexually immoral, murderers, idol worshippers, or liars. Proverbs 27:12 (NLT) says: "A prudent person foresees danger and takes precautions. The simpleton goes blindly on and suffers the consequences."

The true love of God in the life of Christians produces genuine worship from the heart of the believers to God. The love of God

empowers Christians to live according to God's will. True worshippers are Christians who love and fear God. Without a genuine love
for God the Father and people, is a life of hypocrisy. Christians
should love one another. That is the spiritual mandate, no matter
the denomination, because the church of the living God is one. The
church of the living God is one as there are no two heavens, but
one heaven where the saints of God will reign with Jesus Christ.
Practicing the love of God is living in godliness because in God's
kingdom it is only the love of God that reigns and rules there.
Followers of Jesus Christ have to show they truly love people they
can see before claiming they love God. A Christian who claims that
he or she loves God and hates a fellow Christian is a liar. 1 John
4:19–21 (NLT) says:

> We love each other because he loved us first. If someone says,
> "I love God," but hates a fellow believer, that person is a liar;
> for if we don't love people we can see, how can we love God,
> whom we cannot see? And he has given us this command:
> Those who love God must also love their fellow believers.

CHAPTER 4

Epilogue

§

LIVING IN GODLINESS IS A lifestyle for all believers. They demonstrate this in their actions, by obeying God at all times and speaking the truth according to God's Word. These Christians are prudent in their daily conduct by abiding in God's Word to live in godliness. They realize they are accountable to God for their lifestyle.

Living in God's righteousness is the spiritual mandate for the church of the living God, to set an example on how Christians should live. Trying to engage in the things that are not approved by God is going against His values. The church is encouraged to turn away from evil and follow the instructions of God, to live blameless lives, and to pursue godliness, which is a pleasing lifestyle that honors God. According to 2 Corinthians 7:1 (NLT), "Because we have these promises, dear friends, let us cleanse ourselves from everything that can defile our body or spirit. And work toward complete holiness because we fear God."

Apostle Paul continues to expound on the principle of living a godly lifestyle. He is addressing the church as a body of Christ, which is also applicable to the church of today on how Christians should conduct their lives. Living in godliness is the pillar and the ground of truth. Living in godliness is the true foundation for Christianity. According to 1 Timothy 3:15–16 (KJV):

But if I tarry long, that thou mayest know how thou oughtest to behave thyself in the house of God, which is the church of the living God, the pillar and ground of the truth. And without controversy great is the mystery of godliness: God was manifest in the flesh, justified in the spirit, seen of angels, preached unto the Gentiles, believed on in the world, received up in Glory.

Paul recognized the importance of personal engagement in discussing this concept. He is unfortunately not in the vicinity to enable him to engage them as a group. He has heard that nonbelievers may have infiltrated the church to cause controversy among the brethren on godliness and the mysteries therein. However, he knew and is confident that the "Word" has been deposited in them.

Apostle Paul is here intimating the church about his imminent coming to meet with them, which now appears to be delayed. Pending his eventual visit to the church, he is reminding them of the godly behaviors expected from them and emphasizing the role of the church as the pillar and ground of the truth as ordained by the living God through Jesus Christ.

The concept of godliness is a mystery but not in contention. Here, Apostle Paul was discussing the qualities of a leader in the church, specifically the position of the bishop and deacons. The thrust of his discussion is that bishops and deacons and their families should live blameless lives, godly and holy lives. This is so because the one who called them is holy, and that is Jesus Christ.

Apostle Paul then went on to further describe godliness in relation to Jesus Christ. Apostle Paul alluded to the common thinking in the society that there was controversy over godliness being mysterious. He wanted to dispel the notion that the godliness being mysterious is controversial. He emphatically said there was no controversy because Jesus Christ, who came down in the form of flesh, was real. He dwelt among the people, seen of them, and preached to them. Not only did all see Jesus Christ, He also preached to the Gentiles, and the world believed in Him. The spirit of God worked mightily in him and was seen by all.

There is therefore no controversy about His holiness and that is what is expected from the church leadership. Jesus Christ completed his assignment on reconciling human beings to God the Father while ***living a godly and holy life***. He was seen and witnessed by angels and humanity and was received up in glory.

Through Jesus Christ and powered by the Holy Spirit, Christians can live in godliness. God is willing to help any individual who comes to Him with a genuine heart. There is therefore no excuse for living in an ungodly lifestyle According to 1 Corinthians 6:9–10 (NLT):

> Don't you realize that those who do wrong will not inherit the Kingdom of God? Don't fool yourselves. Those who indulge in sexual sin, or who worship idols, or commit adultery, or are male prostitutes, or practice homosexuality, or are thieves, or greedy people, or drunkards, or are abusive, or cheat people—none of these will inherit the Kingdom of God.

The Word of God is very loud and clear that those who continue to indulge in a lifestyle of sin will not inherit the kingdom of God. God's standard is absolute for all because it has eternal value. Living in godliness is possible through Jesus Christ because of the grace of God.

That does not mean Christians don't make mistakes. The Bible is addressing that members of the church of the living God should live a lifestyle of godliness and not to be involved in willful and deliberate sins. Even when a Christian is involved in any kind of sin, there is room for repentance to obtain God's mercy. God's Word is that rebellion and disobedient individuals who refuse to repent will not have any part in His kingdom.

The grace of God is not an excuse for careless and inappropriate style of living. Genuine repentance is the key to living in godliness. Your personal relationship with God is what counts as a follower of Christ. Now is the time to hear the voice of God to repent from willful and deliberate sins. Jesus Christ is calling everyone who has not truly repented to repent from any kind of sin. Repentance and God's mercy is for the living person alone, not the dead.

God is patiently waiting for you to come to Him. The Lord's coming is imminent. The Church is reminded again about the need for Christ followers to live a godly and holy lifestyle. The Lord's patience should not be taken for granted because He truly wants His people to be saved. Repentance and the coming of the Lord should be frequently preached from the pulpit, as the apostles did during their time. They were going around the churches to remind the Christians on how to live their lives in Christ and not for themselves.

Christians should be on their guard for the god of self, who has held some people in bondage because these individuals promote and emphasize themselves instead of stressing the need for God's Word to live in godliness. Christians should try to uphold and encourage one another spiritually. The Word of God should be preached in the way it is stated, to produce true disciples who are faithful and committed to the work of God for spiritual uplift and genuine zeal for God.

Genuine zeal for God directs Christians toward living in godliness, not to twist the scripture for personal gain. The Word of God is profitable for living in godliness because God's Word reproves, corrects, and instructs God's people for righteous living and to prepare the church of the living God for the coming of the Lord Jesus Christ. Any message that does not encourage righteous living and prepares God's people for the coming of the Lord is false and misleading. According to 2 Timothy 3:16–17 (KJV), "All scripture is given by inspiration of God, and is profitable for doctrine, for reproof, for correction, for instruction in righteousness: That the man of God may be perfect, thoroughly furnished unto all good works."

The Bible is the moral absolute for living in godliness. The Word of God corrects, reproves, and instructs the church of the living God on how to live in godliness. The Lord gave me His Word on February 2, 2017, to the church from Galatians 6:7–10 (KJV), and it says, "Be not deceived; God is not mocked for whatever a man soweth, that shall he also reap. For he that soweth to his flesh shall of the flesh reap corruption, but he that soweth to the Spirit shall of the Spirit reap life everlasting. And let us not be weary in well doing: for in due season we shall reap, if we faint not. As we have therefore opportunity, let us do good unto all men, especially unto them who are of the household of faith."

Living a deceptive life is very dangerous and misleading because it can lead people away from God. God sees every motive and knows the thought of every person. Every evil seed sown has consequences if there is no repentance. Evil seed makes room for motives that are ungodly through manipulation, sowing seeds of discord, and evil practices. Manipulation is one kind of evil seed that is used to achieve selfish goals. Teaching the Word of God to manipulate audiences is evil and deceptive because there is no power in such words to save lives. The godly preach the Word of God for people to be saved and live a righteous life. Colossians 2:8 (NLT) says, "Don't let anyone capture you with empty philosophies and high-sounding nonsense that come from human thinking and from the spiritual powers of this world, rather than from Christ."

Living in godliness is a moral norm for all believers in the Lord Jesus Christ. Godliness should not be a controversy for believers in the Lord Jesus Christ because that is the spiritual mandate for Christians to live in God's will. God had already made provision in His grace to live a godly lifestyle by the power of the Holy Spirit. God approves of all Christians living a pleasing lifestyle. Doing the will of God is the foundation of living in godliness. When Jesus

Christ is not the center of His followers' lives, practicing godliness will be very challenging and difficult.

When Christians rely on self and strength, they will lose focus. Reading God's Word daily will help a Christian to grow and increase in the knowledge of God and to gain understanding. The Word of God is the spiritual manual for believers in the Lord Jesus Christ to navigate a spiritual journey. Christians are encouraged to study God's Word in order for them to live their full spiritual potential. Please, my brothers and sisters, don't settle for less other than to live the plan of God for your life. By living in an ungodly lifestyle, you are settling for less.

Living in godliness is a lifestyle of total dependence on God through Jesus Christ. Living in godliness requires perseverance and endurance to follow Jesus Christ at all costs with determination to be a lover of God. Living in godliness is to treasure God's Word daily. Matthew 6:21 (KJV) says, "For where your treasure is, there will your heart be also."

If knowing Jesus is just using His name to get fame or as a means to an end, then you need to rethink so you can know God personally. Daniel 11:32b (KJV) reads, "But the people that do know their God shall be strong and do exploits."

When you know God personally, you will serve Him with sincerity from your heart. Then the Holy Spirit will help you to live in godliness, recognizing the kingship of Jesus Christ and His lordship over your life. Living in godliness will involve quality time spent in the presence of God. Living in godliness is a lifestyle of thanking God always for His Grace and the privilege to be a follower of Jesus Christ. God's desire is for His children to have followership with Him because He needs our totality.

It is a great privilege to have intimacy with God through His Word and prayer. Living in godliness is growing into spiritual maturity by enjoying every moment and fellowship with God. Living in godliness shows the evidence of a changed life; a life in godliness is Christ-like.

1 Timothy 6:3–21(NIV)

"If anyone teaches otherwise and does not agree to the sound instruction of our Lord Jesus Christ and to godly teaching, they are conceited and understand nothing. They have an unhealthy interest in controversies and quarrels about words that result in envy, strife, malicious talk, evil suspicions and constant friction between people of corrupt mind, who have been robbed of the truth and who think that godliness is a means to financial gain.

But godliness with contentment is great gain. For we brought nothing into the world, and we can take nothing out of it. But if we have food and clothing, we will be content with that. Those who want to get rich fall into temptation and a trap and into many foolish and harmful desires that plunge people into ruin and destruction. For the love of money is a root of all kinds of evil. Some people, eager for money, have wandered from the faith and pierced themselves with many griefs.

But you, man of God, flee from all this, and pursue righteousness, godliness, faith, love, endurance and gentleness. Fight the good fight of the faith. Take hold of the eternal life to which you were called when you made your good confession in the presence of many witnesses. In the sight of God, who gives life to everything, and of Christ Jesus, who while testifying before Pontius Pilate made the good confession, I charge you to keep this command without spot or blame until the appearing of our Lord Jesus Christ, which God will bring about in his own time—God, the blessed and only Ruler, the King of kings and Lord of lords, who alone is immortal and who lives in unapproachable light, whom no one has seen or can see. To him be honor and might forever. Amen.

Command those who are rich in this present world not to be arrogant nor to put their hope in wealth, which is so uncertain, but to put their hope in God, who richly provides us with everything for our enjoyment. Command them to do good, to be rich in good deeds, and to be generous and willing to share. In this way they will lay up treasure for themselves as a firm foundation for the coming age, so that they may take hold of the life that is truly life.

Timothy, guard what has been entrusted to your care. Turn away from godless chatter and the opposing ideas of what is falsely called knowledge, which some have professed and in so doing have departed from the faith.

Grace be with you all."

NOTES

NOTES

Notes

NOTES

NOTES

Notes

NOTES

Notes